Revised Edition

Class Meetings

Young Children Solving Problems Together

Emily Vance

National Association for the Education of Young Children
Washington, DC

National Association for the Education of Young Children
1313 L Street NW, Suite 500
Washington, DC 20005-4101
202-232-8777 • 800-424-2460
www.naeyc.org

NAEYC Books

Chief Publishing Officer
Derry Koralek

Editor-in-Chief
Kathy Charner

Director of Creative Services
Edwin C. Malstrom

Managing Editor
Mary Jaffe

Senior Editor
Holly Bohart

Senior Graphic Designer
Malini Dominey

Associate Editor
Elizabeth Wegner

Editorial Assistant
Ryan Smith

Through its publications program, the National Association for the Education of Young Children (NAEYC) provides a forum for discussion of major issues and ideas in the early childhood field, with the hope of provoking thought and promoting professional growth. The views expressed or implied in this book are not necessarily those of the Association or its members.

Permissions

Musical Shapes and Frozen Bean Bag on page 35 are adapted, by permission, from W. Kreidler & S.T. Whittall, *Adventures in Peacemaking: A Conflict Resolution Activity Guide for Early Childhood Educators*, 2nd ed. (Cambridge, MA: Educators for Social Responsibility, and Boston: Work/Family Directions, 1999), 4–31, 4–33.

Do You See What I See? on page 35 is adapted, by permission, from W.J. Kreidler, *Teaching Conflict Resolution Through Children's Literature* (New York: Scholastic Professional Books, 1994), 70.

The box "Recording Kind Acts" on page 39 is adapted, by permission, from P. Whitin, "Kindness in a Jar," *Young Children* 56 (September 2001): 18–22.

Parts of "Children's Books for Building Conflict Resolution Skills" on pages 48–89 are adapted, by permission, from N. Carlsson-Paige & D.E. Levin, *Before Push Comes to Shove: Building Conflict Resolution Skills With Children* (St. Paul, MN: Redleaf, 1998), 87–89.

Photo Credits

Copyright © Ellen Senisi: 21, 41, 55; Susan Woog Wagner/© NAEYC: Cover, 17, 23, 29, 33, 61; Richard Graessle/© NAEYC: 37; Barbara Bent/© NAEYC: 38; courtesy of the author: 1, 9, 13

Credits

Children's art is courtesy of the author

Contributing Editor: Lacy Thompson

Cover Design: Edwin Malstrom

Library of Congress Control Number: 2013947530

ISBN: 978-1-938113-00-0

NAEYC Item 172

Contents

Foreword

Imagine a world where class meetings are the norm. Every child has the opportunity to learn problem-solving and conflict management skills in a structured, nurturing way that is woven right into the school day. Every child learns to handle sensitive communication, respect feelings and personal truth, recognize and honor differences, appreciate himself or herself and others, and work and play with others constructively. Every child develops these innate abilities in an environment of safety and comfort—building self-confidence and trust and developing relationships and a sense of community. These children are well-prepared to contribute deeply of themselves, as engaged and fulfilled members of society.

The significance of beginning this work in early childhood cannot be overstated. While much has been accomplished through peer mediation programs, these tend to target middle school and older students. Often these are short-term training programs outside the curriculum, specifically focused on bullying and other conflict management skills. Educators wanting to implement a more comprehensive approach to developing students' communication skills may be challenged by curriculum demands, competing priorities, and funding limitations.

Emily Vance offers a holistic, embedded approach that provides a solid foundation for all children to discover and explore their interests and abilities safely and fully—from preschool onward. With effort and minimal expense, a successful class meeting culture can be established within the existing infrastructure of every classroom. Why wait? Through class meetings, children learn to share their experiences and collaborate with peers productively. Throughout their education, the power of individual and collective creative endeavor is reinforced.

The long-term potential for this systemic approach is very positive indeed. Imagine the cumulative impact of millions of individuals equipped with this educational experience. World peace does not seem so far-fetched a notion.

Imagine.

—Sara L. Krusenstjerna, Esq.
Creative Consulting

Introduction

This book is written *by* a teacher *for* teachers. Too often education programs are developed by people who do not work in the classroom and who have not considered all the dynamics of using their methods in a school setting over a long period of time. The programs may look good in theory but prove difficult in practice.

I have found the approach presented in this book to be practical and effective. It is highlighted with examples from my early

childhood teaching practice of more than 35 years. You know the children in your class best—use your own good judgment in adapting and applying these strategies and approaches.

A word of advice about beginning to use the information in this book: class meetings are not something you try once a week for a few weeks and then decide whether they are working. I have found that the benefits from using class meetings often appear several weeks or months after beginning their use. To use class meetings effectively, make a commitment to allow time for regular class meetings to support positive changes in class and individual communication and problem-solving skills. I recommend using class meetings daily for at least three months to reach a level of comfort and skill in facilitating the meetings and to give the children time to become familiar with the routines and processes involved in this forum for classroom communication. This extended period of time provides enough opportunity to observe the effects of class meetings on the classroom climate and interactions. For class meetings, as with all good classroom management programs, patience, commitment, and consistency nurture long-term results.

Class meetings have many different names and take just as many forms. Some teachers call them group time, gathering time, community circle, or morning meeting. Meetings may tie in to specific aspects of the curriculum or offer community-building activities or routines to ease young children's daily transitions from home to school. Although the class meeting format outlined in this book has features touching on all these themes, the focus in this book is on conflict resolution, co-constructing problem-solving strategies, and making the classroom a safe, positive environment so that children can channel their energy into constructive interactions and learning.

The Components of a Class Meeting

Class meetings have four major components:

1. Opening
2. Acknowledgments
3. Problem solving
4. Closing

The exciting thing about class meetings is that they are always different and unique, and they can vary according to time constraints, the children's concerns, and the teacher.

From my experience, I became a believer in class meetings when I observed children beginning to use problem-solving strategies *outside* the meetings, depending less on adults, and using positive language with each other—stepping-stones on the path to healthy self-esteem and respect for others. Class meetings help create a safe environment for everyone. These elements can transform a group of individual children into a real community of learners.

What Are Class Meetings?

The following class meeting with kindergartners illustrates how we hear and perceive differing events and the importance of learning ways to clarify and communicate to work together.

Teacher: Hello, class, and thank you for coming to our class meeting. Does anyone have an acknowledgment they would like to share?

Saul: I want to acknowledge Terrell for playing with me.

Teacher: Terrell, do you remember playing with Saul?

Terrell: Yes.

Teacher: What were you playing?

Terrell: We were playing tag at recess.

Teacher: Did you have fun?

Terrell: Yes!

Teacher: Saul, did you have any problems when you were playing tag?

Saul: No, it was fun.

Teacher: Saul and Terrell, how did you keep from having problems?

Saul: We took turns.

Terrell: Yeah and if he bumped me, he said, "Sorry."

Teacher: Great! Terrell, what do you say to Saul to let him know you appreciate his acknowledgment?

Terrell: Thank you, Saul.

Teacher: Okay, let's move on. Does anyone have a problem they would like to work on? [Maya raises her hand.] Okay, Maya, tell us about your situation.

Maya: Dustin called you (the teacher) a cow.

Teacher: Dustin, do you remember this happening?

Dustin: I did not!

Maya: Yes, you did.

Dustin: I did not! (louder)

Maya: You did too. (softly)

Dustin: I did not call her a cow. I said she looks like a cow! (loudly)

Teacher: (After taking a deep breath and looking down toward the floor, I notice that the print design in the outfit I am wearing has big black spots surrounded with white.) Dustin, is it possible that the outfit I am wearing reminded you of a cow?

Dustin: (Jumping up from across the circle and running toward me) Yes! I love you, Ms. Vance! (With that he gives me a big hug and sits down next to me for the remainder of the meeting.)

Prior to this class meeting, Maya had not verbally shared in class meetings. In addition, Dustin presented challenging behavior with his classmates. Maya's concern for my well-being prompted her to take action and empowered her to share her concern.

As a result of his experience in this class meeting, Dustin began to lead some class meetings, listening attentively to his classmates, and asking questions of his peers. There was a significant change in his overall behavior. During subsequent class

> Often I substitute the word *problem* with alternative word choices such *as issue, situation,* or *dilemma* to increase the class shared community vocabulary and to counteract negative associations many have with the word *problem.*

meetings throughout the year, Maya continued listening respectfully and sharing acknowledgments.

In the scenario with Maya, her previous experience with class meetings empowered her to speak up. During class meetings, teachers are required to make on-the-spot decisions based on the students' backgrounds, school protocols, and the teacher's knowledge and experience with the students and parents. This dialogue presents how one teacher manages a class meeting, which often highlights the importance of flexibility.

Imagine how you would feel if someone called you a cow or said something that hurt your feelings. How would your response affect your ability to concentrate? If you were given an opportunity to talk—to share your feelings, hear responses by others, and arrive at a solution—consider the difference it would make in your day. Class meetings give children the opportunity to develop their oral language and communication skills. Children experience the problem-solving process along with the support of their peers and teacher. As they discuss the problem, children discover a variety of options they can choose to use for their personal conflict resolution.

Class meetings can have a positive effect on the school day. They offer a forum for group problem solving with the children solving the problems and the teacher facilitating. They provide children an opportunity to speak out about their feelings in a nonthreatening environment, where thoughts and views can be expressed without fear of ridicule, finger-pointing, or recriminations. They help make school a place that is emotionally safe for children. This feeling of safety enhances group trust along with children's ability to concentrate and learn.

During a class meeting a child who wants or needs to address a conflict presents her view of the problem. The other children involved in the incident are invited to give their perspectives. With guidance from the teacher and suggestions from other class members, the children work together to explore problem-solving strategies. From their experiences

This is how Gail McClurg explains to her kindergartners the concept of a class meeting (which she calls community meeting):

> I introduce it very simply as a time when we can talk about our lives together in such a way that everyone can feel safe and have a chance to speak about the things on our minds. When there is a problem, we can help each other look for a solution. I make it clear as the first meetings proceed that this is a time to problem solve, not to judge. We really need to listen to each other, and everyone is important. (1998, 31)

in class meetings, children develop a sense of trust and learn to value honesty, to respect feelings, and to care about each other.

Creating a Sense of Community

Respect is essential to ensure a safe, positive environment in class meetings—and in the classroom and other school settings. It is the foundation upon which a caring and trusting atmosphere is built. The teacher communicates respect through her words, and more importantly, her actions. A teacher's first step toward creating a respectful classroom is modeling respect in her own interactions with the children. When the teacher models openness, empathy, and thoughtfulness in helping children resolve their differences, even very young children begin to learn to settle their problems responsibly and respectfully.

A parent observes: "At the class meetings I've seen, the children clearly demonstrated that rather than one or two, there might be four or six or seven points of view, all valid, that describe a given event. Once those points of view were understood, the children seemed prepared to move on to solutions and finally actions."

Discussing the value of class meetings, Styles (2001) writes,

Class meetings unify the class—as conflicts in the class are resolved and feelings are shared, friction is reduced. At this point, the class begins to function as a community, working together toward goals and showing support for all members. Students feel a sense of belonging to the group, and the tone in the classroom becomes very positive and caring. (9)

The flexible format of class meetings and the sense of community foster a number of positive social behaviors. In meetings children practice showing respect for one another by taking turns and listening attentively. Jalongo (2008) defines listening: "Listening is the process of taking in information through the sense of hearing and making meaning of what was heard" (2008, 12).

As they hear and consider others' perspectives, children become more capable of seeing beyond their own developmentally appropriate egocentric view. Students become familiar with feeling empathy. Recognizing and expressing appreciation for others' constructive words and actions is another benefit enhancing each child's social competence while fostering communication and a positive classroom climate. Also, children learn how to evaluate ideas and develop reasonable, respectful solutions.

8

Practicing problem solving and resolving conflicts in the group, children bring this experience with them and use it in their daily interactions, applying the strategies and the vocabulary learned in class meetings and extending their use in other contexts. Dombro, Jablon, and Stetson encourage teachers to maximize everyday communications with Powerful Interactions defined as "those in which you intentionally connect with the child while at the same time saying or doing something to guide the child's learning a small step forward" (2011, 13).

Using Active Listening

Active listening is an important part of class meetings. It includes the actual listening process between the teacher and children that occurs each time a child speaks, and it also includes the follow-up of the listening techniques of encouraging, restating, reflecting, and summarizing (Decker 1988). Encouragement by the teacher promotes continued conversation. Restating reflects the ability to understand what a child says through the use of feedback and mirroring information. Reflecting focuses on how children are feeling. Summarizing encompasses the key ideas voiced as a way of extending the conversation.

Respect

In my classroom we have one major, overarching guideline and that is to show and maintain respect. Over the years, I have found that once the concept of respect has been established among the students, other rules or guidelines lead back to this concept. When challenges occur, I encourage the children to pause and guide them by asking "Are you showing respect?" or encouraging them to ask themselves "Am I showing respect?" These questions serve as a way to reflectively begin the problem-solving process and also give the children and teacher a moment to calm down if emotions are high. If children are noticeably having difficulty concentrating on the problem solving and continue to show signs of emotional stress, we may change and do some deep breathing and relaxation exercises.

The first weeks of class meetings are a wonderful time to introduce the topic of respect. I invite children to participate in an open discussion on what showing respect means. A response to this question involves abstract critical thinking. It is important to take time and not rush young children's responses. Often they will give personal examples such as "He hitted me." Sometimes children look as though they are unsure and do not respond. I may pose another question to give another perspective, for example, "If you hit someone with a block, is that showing respect?" Most of the time children are keen on identifying what respect is not. This provides children an opportunity to share in the discussion about behavior that may not be respectful. Over the next few weeks, continued group conversations can highlight the meaning of respect. Next, we begin building our group definition using the children's thoughts and contributions from various discussions. This then moves toward creating a group definition of respect. The children often suggest that respect is caring, not hurting others, feeling good, and playing nicely. Once we co-construct this group definition and the term has begun to be commonly used within the classroom, I introduce three types of respect to extend children's understanding of the concept.

- Respect for the environment
- Respect for others
- Respect for self

I begin with respect for the environment, which is more tangible and easier for young children to grasp. I then group environment into two categories, outdoor and

Active listening in a class meeting presents a unique opportunity for the teacher to model authentic interest by listening to the children express their ideas and responding from a neutral, engaged perspective while conveying respect and acceptance. This can be accomplished, as demonstrated in the following example, through teacher-led questions that show a willingness to listen and be flexible (Vance 2009).

indoor. I generally talk about the outdoor areas with the trees, plants, mountains, birds, animals, air, and water. We may even go outside to have the class meeting. This can lead to a discussion during which children can identify the different components of the outdoor area that they respect such as the grass, air, or playground equipment. We may examine misused play equipment or trash lying on the playground, and I will ask, "Is this showing respect? What can we do to help show respect when we are outdoors?" During many meetings we have had discussions about hanging on trees or climbing young trees with fragile branches. Together, we establish that pulling off leaves or hanging on tree branches may cause damage to the young tree. In order for the tree to grow, we must show respect and leave it alone. We follow this outdoor experience by going inside and touring the classroom activity areas, sharing ways that we can show respect within the classroom environment to the furniture, plants, supplies, books, and materials. This leads nicely to the second category, respect for others.

The children are often excited to offer ways that they show respect for other children, family, and friends. They may suggest ways they show respect for others by being helpful or being a friend. Children enjoy sharing ways they can support others. We may talk about tearing up someone else's paper or grabbing a crayon or paint brush to determine if this is respectful. When we have the concept of respect established, we can share ways to support one another. I use general role-playing situations such as, "What would you do if someone took the blocks you wanted to use?" Then I have two children role-play what would be respectful so other children in the group can see effective ways to strengthen and reinforce the idea of respect.

Of the three types, respect for self appears to be the most challenging for young children to understand as it also includes and involves using the other two types of respect; showing respect for the environment and for others also has benefits for the person showing respect. Children become aware that when they do kind deeds for others and the environment it also has an impact on them. For example, when a child acknowledges other children's positive behaviors, this leads to a continuation of these types of behaviors.

Finally, it is important for teachers to model respect in voice, tone, and body language when working with children. In class meetings children watch, learn, and practice these important social skills as we interact with our colleagues and other children.

Teacher: Remember the other day we were giving acknowledgments? Does someone remember what an acknowledgment is?

Mina: (Begins singing "Five Little Hotdogs") Five little hot dogs frying in the pan, the grease got hot and one went bam! (A group of children join in singing along with Mina.)

Teacher: Wow, you know a great song! Remember the other day when we were talking about acknowledgments?

Mina: (nods yes)

A willingness to listen and be flexible supports a sense of a classroom community.

Promoting Cognitive Development

Beyond promoting respectful interactions and practicing communication skills, class meetings are valuable for developing children's critical reasoning and problem-solving skills. To describe a problem situation to other children and the teacher, the child needs to recall events in sequence. He has to put into words what he recalls, enhancing his language skills. Nielsen expands this idea through her discussion on receptive oral language development, which is when a child

- Responds appropriately to simple questions
- Recalls facts, details, and sequence of events in stories
- Focuses attention on speaker
- Listens to and engages in several exchanges of conversation with others (adapted from 2006, 7)

Nielsen also shares that expressive oral language development involves:

- Communicating nonverbally through gestures, movements, and expressions
- Using language to express needs, ideas . . . feelings
- Participating in informal conversations about experiences and following conversation rules (adapted from 2006, 7)

She continues with the interconnection between oral language and social emotional development, stating that the interaction "demonstrates growing understanding of how their actions affect others and begins to accept consequences of their actions" (2006, 12).

Glasser writes,

Another advantage of class meetings is the confidence that a child gains when he states his opinion before a group. In life there are many opportunities to speak for oneself. The more we teach children to speak clearly and thoughtfully, the better we prepare them for life. When a child can speak satisfactorily for himself, he gains a confidence that is hard to shake. (1969, 144)

Remember in the opening vignette on page 5 how Maya spoke up for her teacher? As a result of her experience with class meetings, she was able to raise an issue at a class meeting.

By listening and trying to understand what happened—often from more than one perspective—the children can use and extend their receptive language skills. Because children are typically quite interested in problems brought to a class meeting, they make a great effort to comprehend what is said and envision the events they hear described.

These highly engaging experiences with language and interaction are very useful to children learning a second language. Moreover, both language comprehension and formation of internal representations of things and events (often from written or spoken words) are critical skills throughout schooling. Beyond these vital capabilities, class meetings challenge children to practice and extend other higher-order thinking skills, such as

• Drawing on long-term memory

• Brainstorming possible strategies and solutions

• Using analytical thinking

• Evaluating solutions from various perspectives

• Putting together these steps in problem solving

Fostering Skills for Life

Class meetings are beneficial for many age groups, from preschool through kindergarten and the primary grades. (With toddlers and 2-year-olds, these concepts and vocabulary can be introduced when a situation arises with two or more children—for more information on mini meetings, see p. 55 in Chapter 5). In school, in play, and at home, children draw upon the social and cognitive skills honed in class meetings. Problem solving, strategizing, negotiating, analyzing, speaking in a group, appreciating other perspectives—when these skills are introduced early in life and reinforced in preschool, kindergarten, and the primary years, children internalize them for use throughout their life span. They are abilities valued not only in the school setting but also later in the workplace and in adults' personal interactions and relationships.

DeVries and Kohlberg place the importance of class meetings—their role in building a caring community by developing cognitive abilities and promoting strong social skills and values—at a higher level, outside the classroom setting and in the larger society:

> By building a just community, teachers are engaged in the most important task of education: helping children develop the intellectual, social, and moral competence, the 'habits of thought and action,' on which the survival of social democracy and individual human welfare so vitally depend. (1990, 181)

DeVries and Zan (1994) highlight the perspective that children must construct a moral understanding from the raw material of their day-to-day social interactions.

3

The Four Components of Class Meetings

Group time, gathering time, "gathering around" (Grant & Davis 2012, 129), morning meeting, community circle, or community meeting—class meetings have many different names and take just as many forms. Meetings may tie in to specific aspects of the curriculum or offer community-building activities or routines to ease young children's daily transitions from home to school. Although the class meeting format outlined in this book has features touching on all these themes, the focus in this book is on conflict resolution, problem solving, and making the classroom a safe, positive environment so that children can channel their energy into constructive interactions and learning.

The following pages present a class meeting framework or scaffolding consisting of four major components—opening, acknowledgments, problem solving, and closing—which have proven helpful when beginning class meetings. However, teachers need not adhere rigidly to this format. These components can be used as a starting framework. Feel free to borrow and adapt elements to fit your classroom needs and the needs of the children. The exciting thing about class meetings is that they are always different and unique, and they vary according to time constraints, the children's concerns, and the teacher.

Opening

The teacher or a designated student calls the children together for class meetings, inviting them to form a circle so that each child can see everyone else. First- or second-graders may prefer to place their chairs in a circle, while younger children can sit on the floor. Children in preschool programs range in age from 3 to 5 years, and it is important to note that giving them the opportunity to select class meetings from a variety of activities is preferable. In the beginning there may be only one or two children to select attending the class meetings. This may last for several weeks before other students choose to attend. (See the sidebar on age ranges in class meetings.)

Providing quiet, self-initiated choices such as puzzles, the book corner, painting, block building, dress-up, science investigation, or playdough allows the teacher the freedom to focus on working with the class meeting group. I always sit with a clear view of all children throughout the classroom when doing this. I have found that with young preschoolers, it may take several weeks for them to select coming to the class meeting. However, this usually changes when the children get an opportunity to be listened to and gain self-confidence in their problem solving. It is also interesting that at times children appear to be engaged with classroom activities in other areas of the room but will then make comments from there regarding the class meeting conversation.

Sometimes when children are engaged in other classroom activities, such as snack time, I begin singing the following song or one that is familiar as a transition

Age Ranges in Class Meetings

Many preschool classrooms combine 3- to 5-year-old children within their classroom groups. Younger children (3-year-olds) often take the initiative and show interest by attending the class meetings before their older classmates. These initial class meetings may be the first encounters young children have in a group setting. Keeping these first gatherings within an age-appropriate timeframe of less than 10–15 minutes and presenting the children the opportunity to be actively listened to by the teacher over time offer a familiarity with the group dynamics and the results these class meeting discussions provide. These early class meetings also introduce the important communication skills of turn-taking, listening to others, and making acknowledgments. Focusing these early class meetings on incorporating these skills serves as a way of preparing the children for the ensuing larger group meetings that may include a variety of age ranges.

and signal that a class meeting is about to begin (sing to the tune of "If You're Happy and You Know It"):

> Come and join us on the rug, it's gathering time
>   (or class meeting time) [clap, clap]
>
> Come and join us on the rug, it's gathering time [clap, clap]
>
> Come and join us on the rug,
>
> Come and join us on the rug,
>
> Come and join us on the rug, it's gathering time. [clap, clap]

Other times when the children are playing outdoors, I call out "Gathering time" (or "community circle" or "class meeting!") and they take up the cry, passing along the message and heading inside at a run. Class meetings can quickly become a favorite time. I like to open with a familiar song or two such as "The More We Get Together," "Row, Row, Row Your Boat," or "Friends, One, Two, Three," then move on to a brief activity or game, such as finger plays for young children or looking at a picture or reading a short book to help the children come together as a group. Harris and Fuqua tell us,

> This is a time for shared rituals that give children meaning as a specific, special group of people. Gathering together is a time to acknowledge the unique contributions of each member of the group. Predictable routines and rituals also provide structure for the day ahead and offer a sense of safety, belonging, and caring for one another. (2000, 44)

Yazigi and Seedhouse (2005) add that the focus is on creating a sense of community and developing social and interactional skills.

Meeting openings are a transition time. Their purpose is to bring the children together, help them practice positive talk, and let go of stressful feelings, tension, and worries so they can concentrate on the day's activities and learning. From time to time, I begin the day with a special morning meeting. Here, children are invited to share about others who are on their minds: a family member, friend, classmate, or perhaps a pet who is sick or whom they miss. As a child reveals a name, they can also make the gesture of placing their special names into the circle by extending their arm forward. Then the children can choose to join hands in a circle, quietly sending thoughts of love and kindness to those named that day or those they are thinking about. By sharing each other's concerns and loving thoughts during this brief activity (lasting 5 to 10 minutes), children experience being listened to by others, releasing emotions, and drawing closer together as a classroom community.

> A teacher says, "The most important part of class meeting is the acknowledgment of appropriate behavior by the children. In my bilingual, multiage classroom, I have seen children acknowledge appropriate behavior in many instances outside the format of class meetings. I have heard children praise and acknowledge as well as voice their own needs to one another."

Later in the day, when another class meeting is held, the children can share and reflect on how they supported each other as a result of the earlier morning activity. This process helps develop empathy and caring among the students.

Acknowledgments

The acknowledgments component of class meetings encourages children to notice others' positive actions and voice their appreciation for another person's thoughtfulness, assistance, or courtesy. Sometimes the words *acknowledgment* and *compliment* are used interchangeably but there is a difference. An *acknowledgment* recognizes a meaningful interaction between people, such as an action by someone who was helpful, considerate, and respectful or one that produced a positive emotion for the child. In contrast, a *compliment* may be just a flattering or pleasing observation about another person as with noting the pretty color of an article of clothing someone wears. Teachers can use an acknowledgment, such as "I noticed that you and Jimmy played together for a long time at the sand table," instead of the frequently heard classroom phrasing, "I like the way you played with Jimmy today." Here the teacher's acknowledgment is identifying and observing the children's positive behavior rather than simply praising them for pleasing her. Acknowledgments provide information without being manipulative or controlling. It is important to note that children are not discouraged from giving compliments but teachers help them distinguish the difference between them and acknowledgments. Depending on the children's age, it may take multiple attempts before they develop this understanding and use the terms in this way. (See "Giving Children Useful Feedback" below.)

Giving Children Useful Feedback

As early childhood teachers, we continually give children feedback. We need to make sure that we do so in ways that are respectful and productive. In recent decades, researchers and expert practitioners have warned against praise that tends to undermine a child's intrinsic motivation—that is, the child's acting for motives or rewards within himself (Brophy 2004; Kohn 2011; Stipek 1998). *Evaluative praise*, such as "Good job" or "You're a really great helper," leads children to look for external proof that they are good or right (Moorman 2001). When teachers make frequent use of evaluative praise with children, they actually may cause children anxiety. Children will think If the teacher can give, the teacher can also take away (Moorman 2001). Staal extends on Moorman's 2001 concept of "evaluative praise" by advising us to proceed with caution as the effects of this kind of praise are temporary (Staal 2008, 28). More recently, Moorman has noted key phrases for teacher talk such as "Next time, please . . . " (Moorman 2003, 36). Teachers can incorporate the phrase "next time" into a question when problem solving. For example, "What do you want to happen next time?" or "Tell us what you'd like to have happen next time." This way, children present a possibility for the future, taking the emphasis off what has happened.

Descriptive feedback, by contrast, notes specifically what children do. A teacher might say, "I noticed the three of you worked together at the computers today" or "Look, the ball went farther when you threw it with one hand." Such feedback helps children focus on what is relevant to the task or situation and not on winning praise from the adult.

Another kind of positive feedback is acknowledgment or *appreciative praise* (Moorman 2001), which often includes the words "I appreciate" or "thank you." For example, a teacher might say to a young child, "Thanks for cleaning up the block area. You've helped get our classroom ready for tomorrow."

Acknowledgments quickly become a crucial part of class-room life. Children do not naturally seem to notice and identify others' constructive actions. Like empathy, sharing, turn taking, and other social skills, recognizing and acknowledging others for their positive actions are skills that must be learned. Once children pick up these skills, acknowledgments are given freely in the classroom and on the playground. Acknowledgments can make a dramatic difference in the classroom climate, and appreciating the positive in situations or people is a habit of mind that works to an individual's advantage throughout life. I have also found that in the beginning weeks of introducing acknowledgments, children ages 3 to 5 will often direct shared acknowledgments to a family member, even when asked to acknowledge someone sitting within our class meeting circle. This seems to be a safe choice because young children are more familiar and comfortable with their families.

From a 7-year-old boy who is a two-year veteran of class meetings: "Whenever Simon does something bad or a few kids aren't following directions, the new teacher makes all of us sit quietly with our hands folded. It isn't fair, and it doesn't make Simon or the other kids do better the next time. She never even tries class meetings."

Children may acknowledge other children or teachers. Their contributions vary, depending on their age and the level of their communication skills. For instance, Jamal, a kindergartner, raised his hand and said, "I want to acknowledge Tiffany for helping me clean up the blocks." Tiffany said, "Thank you, Jamal," letting him know she appreciated the acknowledgment. Eli, a third-grader, said, "Thank you, Mrs. Deal, for helping me with my long division." Georgina, a second-grader, said, "I want to acknowledge Antonio for helping me write the word job in my journal," and Antonio thanked Georgina for the acknowledgment.

The component after acknowledgments is problem solving, the heart of class meetings. Preschools have a wide range of class demographics and ages. Class meetings with 4s and 5s can be too long for very young children to sit through. If you have a multiage class or very young children, at this point in the meeting the youngest children may choose another activity. (For problem-solving strategies with this younger age group, see "Mini Meetings: Solving Problems in Small Groups" on p. 55.)

Problem Solving

The problems most commonly brought to class meetings are interpersonal, especially name-calling, arguments or disagreements, and taking someone's property without permission. Many other interpersonal problems come up regularly—excluding others from play, not taking turns or sharing, and aggressive or bullying behavior, to name a few. When a child brings a problem to a meeting, the first step is gathering information.

When gathering information, a variety of perspectives on an incident are heard and considered, not just the view of the child raising the issue. The children take turns presenting their views. The teacher makes this clear, often repeating this point to reassure children who interrupt that they will have a turn soon. This is a good time to remind children that listening to others talk is a way of showing respect. First, the children involved in the situation are given a chance to speak and share their perspectives. Then depending on time constraints, other classmates are individually given an opportunity to contribute their views and suggestions. Problems are discussed without accusation or judgment, with those involved hopefully taking responsibility for their actions and earnestly seeking resolution.

After a child states his or her concern about a problem or challenging situation, I turn to the child whose problem is being addressed, using the question, "Do you remember this happening?" as a nonthreatening way to gain his or her viewpoint. Together, brainstorm a menu of co-constructed ways to resolve the situation. The child presenting the problem is then given a chance to select one of the suggestions. During the next meeting, check in to find out how that suggestion worked. If the child still expresses a concern, he or she can try another approach.

Resolving Conflicts Without Adults

Children can use five problem-solving steps to attempt to clear up misunderstandings. These steps encourage children to communicate respectfully with each other outside the formal structure of meetings. In many cases they will find that they can reach an agreement without teacher guidance. The following guidelines resulted from class meeting conversations and experiences.

Often a problem can be cleared up when the child in distress uses the first two strategies:

1. **Calm down; take some deep breaths.**
2. **Talk to the person with whom you are having a problem. Use I-feel statements.**

Using I-feel statements is the preeminent problem-solving strategy employed in class meetings. (See "Learning to Use I-Feel Statements" in Chapter 4, p. 40.) Respectful communication is the social skill the teacher fosters when he intercedes in children's disagreements in the classroom or on the playground and when he guides problem solving in meetings. Helping children internalize modes of respectful interaction is key. If talking is not productive, the child can take the next step:

3. **Move away from the other person.**

This should end the disagreement—at least for the moment. (Not all problems need be resolved. Some just naturally fade with the passage of time.)

4. **Find friends to stay or play with if you are feeling unsure or unsafe.**

If these strategies fail to provide relief, and the child wants to pursue a solution, he can take the final step:

5. **Sign up for class meeting.**

Over the course of the school year, through purposeful teacher prompts and the use of teachable moments, these steps will become second nature to children, providing a strong foundation in conflict resolution that they can use throughout life.

Learning to consider problems fairly and constructively is a skill young children acquire over time through daily practice in a respectful and caring environment under the attentive guidance of a patient teacher. Gradually children learn that "the purpose of all discussion is to solve problems, not to find fault or to punish. Experience in solving social problems in a non-fault-finding, nonpunitive atmosphere gives children confidence in themselves as thinking, worthwhile people" (Glasser 1969, 129). The ultimate goal is for children to internalize problem-solving strategies and techniques so they become second nature. Then as problems occur throughout the day, it becomes easier for the children to handle the problems themselves, without adult intervention. (See "Resolving Conflicts Without Adults" on p. 22.)

The child presenting the problem explains her view of the situation. For example, Gabriella, a first-grader, says, "My problem is that Rosa calls me names. It makes me feel bad." The teacher asks Gabriella what steps she took to resolve the issue herself—did she talk to Rosa? Gabriella says, "I asked her to stop, but she didn't." The teacher prompts, "What happened next?" "When she didn't stop, I moved to another part of the playground." The teacher then asks Rosa if she remembers the incident.

Early in the school year, before the concept of the classroom as a safe environment has been well established, some children may not remember or hesitate to talk about their part in a problem for fear they will be reprimanded or punished. They may shy away from answering a question or they may not answer honestly. If Rosa says she remembers the incident, the teacher immediately commends her for her honesty and acknowledges her willingness to help resolve the issue. If Rosa does not remember, the teacher goes back to Gabriella for more information, perhaps asking her when and where the incident occurred.

At this point other classmates will wave their hands in the air, saying, "I saw it. I know about this problem." The teacher can get the perspectives of other classmates as well. However, it is important that the attention stay focused on Gabriella and Rosa, the children directly involved in the problem. The problem is theirs, and discussion and resolution will be most meaningful coming from them. (In "An Unwelcome Kiss," on this page, classmates seek clarification and contribute to the problem-solving process.)

After the circumstances have been clarified, the teacher asks the child presenting the problem to propose a solution. A solution is acceptable when the children directly involved in the problem agree to it. (One time a child referred to the person with the problem as the "problemer." Since then I sometimes refer to children

An Unwelcome Kiss

Liliana has a disagreement on the playground with Daniel, a child from a class that does not hold class meetings. Liliana signs up for class meeting.

When Daniel comes to our classroom for the meeting, I describe our meeting procedures. I tell him how the children involved in a problem explain their views of it. I take extra time to emphasize that each person has a chance to explain what happened without being interrupted.

Liliana speaks first. She says Daniel kissed her on the head and kicked her while they were on the slide. Daniel interrupts Liliana several times, and each time I reassure him that he will have an opportunity to talk.

When it is Daniel's turn to give his view of the incident, he says, "Liliana asked me what I wanted to play. We decided to play chase on the slide. After playing chase for a while, I decided I didn't want to play it anymore, so I pretended to kiss her." Daniel explains he pretended to kiss Liliana by blowing a kiss at her. "Then Liliana hit me with her elbows. So I kicked her."

I thank Daniel for being honest and giving us the information we need. I tell him that by doing so, he lets us know that he is willing to solve the problem. At this point it's important to allow time for children's questions so everyone understands what happened.

Eleni: Liliana, did you hit Daniel?

Liliana: Yes.

Eleni: Daniel, did you kick Liliana?

involved as the "problemer" and the other children as the "problemees.") Gabriella might ask Rosa to give her a hug or to draw a picture for her. If Rosa agrees, Gabriella may say, "My problem is solved." If not, the teacher can ask Rosa to propose a solution. At times this process takes several attempts. However, in most cases, the children involved in a problem select a solution quickly. If necessary the teacher can invite the children in the class to contribute their thoughts. This is a good time to remind the children that solutions must be reasonable, respectful, and related to the problem at hand. At times like this, I often ask the following questions to guide children into a reflection of what it might be like if they were in a similar situation: How would you feel if this happened to you? What would you want others to do?

Not surprisingly, in a class meeting children may arrive at a solution or strategy that does not actually seem to solve the problem. Of course the teacher keeps an eye on how things turn out. If all goes well, she may ask the children if their solution worked

---

Daniel: Yes. She hit me.

Valerie: Liliana, why did you hit Daniel?

Liliana: Because he kissed me.

Alberto: Daniel, did you try to kiss Liliana?

Daniel: Yes, but it wasn't a real kiss.

After these and other questions are answered, the children offer a number of possible solutions:

1. Liliana and Daniel should play away from each other.
2. Liliana and Daniel should shake hands and say sorry.
3. Liliana and Daniel can play on the same side of the playground but not on the same equipment.
4. Daniel should tell Liliana when he doesn't want to play anymore instead of pretending to kiss her.
5. Daniel shouldn't pretend to kiss Liliana.

Liliana and Daniel agree to use solutions 2 and 4 to settle their disagreement. They feel that solution 2 will remind them that they are still friends and solution 4 will help prevent the problem from happening again.

When someone from another class takes part in problem solving, it confirms for children the importance of class meeting and validates their ability to resolve conflicts.

Cristi's Library Dilemma

Every day the first-graders visit the school library. They are divided into four groups, each with a different color library card: red, blue, green, or yellow. To check out books the children place their cards in the appropriate color-coded pocket on a pocket chart. When children are responsible for the checkout procedure, they tend to be more conscientious about it. However, many children forget to return their books the next day.

To help children remember to return their books daily, the school librarian devises an incentive: If everyone in a color group brings back their books three days in a row, each group member can check out a special book bag containing a stuffed animal and a book. Upon hearing this, the children's eyes light up.

Within two weeks, a pattern emerges. All the children in the yellow group return their books consistently and take home the special book bags. None of the children in the other three groups get the book bags.

One day in class meeting, Cristi raises her hand: "I want the kids in my group to remember to bring their books back so we can check out book bags too." Cristi reminds all of the children in the red group to return their books. A few days later, when she realizes her reminder is not working, she suggests to her group that they leave the books in their cubbies overnight so that they will be sure to have them to check in at the library the next day. Not all of the children cooperate. Finally, Cristi brings up the problem again in a class meeting.

Cristi says, "I don't think this is fair. I return my book every day, but because others in my group don't remember, I can't check out a book bag."

I ask Cristi if she would like to talk over this problem with the librarian. She says yes and leaves the meeting to go to the library immediately.

When the librarian hears Cristi's dilemma, she sees the problem and changes the system. As a result, Cristi takes home a book bag regularly.

out. And if things do not appear to go well, the teacher can consider various options when the problem arises again. Sometimes she can do some on-the-spot questioning to elicit problem solving with the children directly involved: What can you do? or How can I help? are questions I have found helpful to use when this occurs. (See "Mini Meetings: Solving Problems in Small Groups" in Chapter 5, on p. 55.) In some cases, the teacher may feel that the class can benefit from hearing what happened and doing some group thinking about another solution that may be more effective than the one first tried.

Occasionally children suggest saying "I'm sorry" as a way to resolve their dilemma. One time when this happened, I remember thinking to myself, "Does saying sorry solve a problem?" I decided to maintain a non-judgmental attitude trusting the children to continue with other possible suggestions for this situation. As it turned out, the two children involved selected to say "sorry" in a genuine way as their solution and, to my surprise, this worked for these children.

Some issues raised in class meetings are not conflicts at all. Sometimes children bring up perceived problem situations that may occur in school. (See "Cristi's Library Dilemma" on p. 26.) In other cases children are concerned with out-of-school problems: "The sidewalk's all broken; that's why Lucy fell down. We've got to fix the sidewalk so kids don't get hurt" (Pelo & Davidson 2000, 40). Such concerns call for the same kinds of problem-solving skills that children develop in class meetings focusing on conflicts. When a class meeting becomes a forum for addressing concerns, it fosters the group's consciousness about the welfare of others. With guidance children feel empowered to address a problem and work toward a reasonable and respectful solution.

As teachers we should keep in mind that not all problems need to be solved. Sometimes children just need to talk about a situation and have their feelings acknowledged. Children need to be heard. McClurg gives this example from a meeting in her kindergarten:

> Brant complained about having a small part in *Jack and the Beanstalk*. Two of his classmates expressed similar disappointment: one said he'd had a hard time accepting the role of the cow, and the other said he'd do his best although his part was small. Brant was able to see that he was not the only one experiencing disappointment, and I had an opportunity to reassure the children that I was keeping track so that eventually everyone would get a major role in one of our plays. (1998, 31)

Closing

After one or two problems are resolved, it is time to close the meeting. The teacher might close by acknowledging students, saying something like, "Juanita, thank you for sharing your idea for solving Jaime's problem today" or "I appreciate how everyone came together today to contribute their ideas and show respect." Or she may want to close the meeting by having the children sing a song or play a game.

Another way to close is to ask the children if anyone solved a problem without the help of adults. Adila, a kindergartner with a year's worth of class meeting experience, recounted this success story:

> One time I was outside and I wanted to play with Safina, Maria, and Solidad. I asked them if I could play with them, and they wouldn't let me. So I went to get Raoul and Maria's older sister Angela to help me. They said some stuff in Spanish to the girls. Then I got to play. I felt good because I got to play and I got my problem solved without any grown-ups.

These are some effective ways to motivate children to carry beyond the classroom the strategies they practiced in class meetings.

Finding Time

Teachers new to the concept of class meetings may feel they barely have time in their busy classroom schedules to cover the curriculum let alone hold daily meetings. However, class meetings create more time for learning rather than using up learning time.

When two children are arguing in a classroom where the children participate in class meetings, the teacher can intervene without disrupting the learning: "Leroy and Elise, I see that you are arguing. You seem to have a problem. Would you agree to put your problem aside for now, and we will discuss it and try to resolve it later in class meeting?"

When children know they will have an opportunity to redress their grievances later in the day, they are able to temporarily set aside their worries and concentrate on learning. The time saved in not stopping to sort out conflicts during classroom activities more than makes up for the time spent in class meetings:

> Over time, children will begin to care for one another, solve their own problems, feel more empowered and more in control of their learning, and come to view all in the community as their "teachers." It will be time well spent. (Harris & Fuqua 2000, 47)

Does this mean that teachers should hold class meetings only when children have a problem? (See "What If We Don't Have a Problem?" on p. 30.) I started out that way but soon learned that it is best to meet regularly—ideally on a daily basis. More frequent meetings serve as reminder for children to practice their problem-solving skills and address issues before they snowball.

If you are just beginning to use class meetings and are weighing the benefits, make a commitment to hold them for at least three months before judging the results. It may take that long for children to incorporate their new social skills, begin to use them regularly, and learn to trust one another. The change in the classroom's social climate will be noticeable.

Many teachers use class meeting times for group learning. Meetings work well for group discussion of, say, math, science, writing, or other projects. By working together in a group, young children learn that there is more than one approach to solving all types of problems. Glasser states,

> There is no reason that teachers cannot use [class meetings] for arithmetic, history, science, and other subjects. Whole-class teaching reduces isolation and failure. . . . The team, for example, is the basis of competitive athletics. But in the class curriculum, where it could be equally effective, it is little used. By treating the whole class as a unit, the same spirit of cooperation can arise as arises on athletic teams. (1969, 143–44)

Class meetings may be as brief as 10 minutes or as long as 30 minutes, depending on the children's ages, the amount of business at hand, the nature of the meeting, and the scheduling demands for the day. Children age 5 and older can come together once a day for a more sustained period of 20 to 30 minutes. For preschoolers, I recommend holding two short class meetings, each 10 to 15 minutes in length, rather than one long one. In my classroom there may be as many as three meetings a day, with the third focusing on end-of-the-day reflections. Because some children arrive later or leave before the end of the day, this ensures that most children have an opportunity to participate.

Class meetings seem to work well around lunchtime. It is a time when morning energy starts to dissipate and children's concentration begins to flag. Holding a class meeting provides a change of pace. Because many problems occur during lunchtime, class meetings can also be effective just after lunch.

Sign-Up

There are many ways to select students to participate in the different components of the class meeting. For example with young children (ages 2 to 3) they can use a personal stamp as a way to identify themselves on a piece of paper. One year, I tried using a white board and the children were so fascinated with trying to write their name with the dry erase marker and then erase it that most times the names got erased and then we had to start over. As observed in the Reggio Emilia schools' use of individual stamps for visual communication, the stamp makes a permanent mark on the paper and that way it is easier to keep track of what is going on. The teacher can also have a class meeting list and children can come to her to have their name added to the list. Or he can just keep a mental note of the children that have participated in the meeting, either giving acknowledgments or presenting problems, and making sure that throughout the week different children get an opportunity to share. It is interesting how quickly young children become aware of the attention they receive and sometimes create ways to hold the spotlight. When this happens I carefully try to select other young children to have a turn and remind the students that part of being a problem solver is being a good listener and giving others a turn.

With older children, a sign-up system helps with classroom organization, so it is clear to children wishing to discuss problems in class meetings in what order their problems will be addressed. Asking preschoolers to raise their hands if they have a problem that needs a resolution works well. The teacher calls on children randomly, making sure that anyone that would like to speak get a turn. Slightly older children practicing their early literacy skills may find signing their names on a class meeting clipboard as problems arise to be very satisfying. Early primary children can use a class meeting agenda book in which they write their names and a brief description of the problem. Or the teacher may have the children themselves decide on a sign-up procedure in a meeting at the beginning of the school year.

•   •   •   •

Opening, acknowledgments, problem solving, and closing— these are the basic components of class meetings in the classroom. Teachers can adapt and use them to work for their classroom needs, their children, and within school expectations. The next chapter describes how to introduce class meetings to the children.

Getting Started

The beginning of the school year, with its inherent excitement and stress, can be overwhelming for children of all ages—meeting new children, becoming reacquainted with familiar ones, saying good-bye to parents, anticipating new routines, becoming comfortable in a new classroom. The concept of class meetings can be introduced gradually, using it first as a vehicle to bring the children together as a group and ease some of the tensions they are experiencing.

Gathering for story time during the first week provides a wonderful way to begin this process. As the children come together to listen to the story, to set the stage, and to prepare children for future meetings, you can begin by

saying, "Next Monday we will have our first class meeting. Class meetings give us a chance to talk together, to learn how to solve problems and how to make school a safe place." The teacher can draw the children into a discussion, by posing a question, for example, "I wonder what it means to you for school to be a safe place?"

Setting the Tone

When talking about what it means to make school safe, young children often tend to think of safety in physical terms. Other behaviors that make children feel unsafe include name-calling, taunting, being laughed at, or being excluded. Having a general discussion focusing on using their words rather than hitting or pushing or bullying provides a means for children to begin participating in this group forum. This is good time to let the children know that school is a place where we consider each other's feelings, where we are able to speak out when something is not right, where we listen respectfully to each other, and where we try to make others feel good about themselves.

A principal notes: "I have watched children in kindergarten through third grade participate in class discussions addressing behavior problems. Solutions to the problems or consequences are addressed, as well as acknowledgments of positive behavior. Children feel they have something to contribute. The resulting social growth may not be measurable on tests but could be far more important to the child than anything else learned in school."

Teachers of older children can lead similar discussions about a safe environment. Although older children may grasp the concept more quickly, having frequent reminders and in-depth exchanges about respectful behavior reinforces the importance of providing a safe environment. At any age children feel safe when they can be honest with each other and with adults without fear of being reprimanded, ridiculed, punished, or treated dismissively. Class meetings serve to establish a level of trust. The teacher can explain the meetings in the context of the children becoming a close-knit, supportive, caring group in which people look out for each other's welfare—a classroom community. Activities outside class meetings also help to create a climate of cooperation and amicable problem solving. (See "Promoting Cooperation and Problem Solving Through Games" on p. 35.)

Promoting Cooperation and Problem Solving Through Games

For most early childhood teachers, helping children learn to resolve conflicts with one another is a major goal. Besides class meetings, there are many ways that teachers weave conflict resolution and problem solving throughout the day and across the curriculum. Because games are interactive and highly engaging, they are excellent for fostering cooperation, problem-solving skills, and certain understandings. Here are a few cooperative games that children love to play.

Musical Shapes

Make large shapes on the floor with masking tape (two circles, two squares, two triangles). Remind children of the names and features of the shapes. Tell them that when the music stops and a shape's name is called out, everyone will try to fit inside that shape. Play music and have the children begin marching; stop the music and name a shape. Encourage and help the children to fit all their classmates into the shape. The shape should be large enough to accommodate all the children but small enough to provide a challenge.

Frozen Bean Bag

Give each child a bean bag and get some lively dancing music ready. Explain to the children that the object of the game is to help each other and to keep moving throughout the song. Show the children how to keep the bean bags on their heads and bend their knees to help a friend pick up a dropped bean bag. Start the music and have the children dance around. If a bean bag slips off a child's head, he or she is frozen and needs another child's help to put it back and become unfrozen.

Do You See What I See?

When playing this game children explore the fact that activities and objects look different depending on the viewer's perspective or interpretation. Stand before the group and pantomime a sample activity; have the children guess the activity (for example, washing windows may look like waving to a friend or erasing the chalkboard). Invite children to act out different activities and discuss what they could be. Make the point that we all see the world differently, and the way we see the world is called our "point of view."

Musical Shapes and Frozen Bean Bag are adapted, by permission, from W. Kreidler & S.T. Whittall, *Adventures in Peacemaking: A Conflict Resolution Activity Guide for Early Childhood Educators*, 2nd ed. (Cambridge, MA: Educators for Social Responsibility, and Boston: Work/Family Directions, 1999), 4–31, 4–33.

Do You See What I See? is adapted, by permission, from W.J. Kreidler, *Teaching Conflict Resolution Through Children's Literature* (New York: Scholastic Professional Books, 1994), 70.

Creating Guidelines

In their first meetings teachers and children can talk about treating others with respect and making the classroom a safe environment. These initial gatherings and discussions are often somewhat chaotic and disorderly, with children speaking out of turn or creating distractions, posing questions such as: "How does it feel when someone else starts talking when you are talking? Do you like it when someone talks when you are sharing?" Teachers can suggest creating some guidelines so children will know when they may speak and when they should listen.

Inviting children to participate in developing the class meeting format is more meaningful for them and they tend to adhere to it when they have taken a role in establishing the guidelines for the class meeting. DeVries and Kohlberg tell about a group of kindergartners who came up with the following rules for good listening:

1. Look at people when they are speaking.

2. Sit still and be silent when someone is speaking.

3. Everyone should get a chance to share.

The next day, when several children did not follow the listening ground rules, the class came up with another:

4. A person will be asked to leave the group if, after one reminder, that person continues not to follow the rules. ([1987] 1990, 159–60)

Other educators prefer to speak of *guidelines* (Gartrell 2014), *agreements* (Pirtle 1998), or *positive action statements* (Moorman 2001) rather than *rules*. Gartrell explains this difference and describes how class meetings define the "encouraging classroom."

> Guidelines—statements of "do's"—frame the standards of conduct for the encouraging classroom. In contrast, rules tend to be stated in the negative—"Don't talk when someone else is." Rules tend to make teachers and children think of the classroom in terms of conformity, defiance, and enforcement. Because the intent of guidelines is to teach rather than punish, guidelines in activities like class meetings are the "gold standard" of the encouraging classroom. During the first class meetings, teachers use the creation of guidelines (through consensus whenever possible) to engender a spirit of community within the class. (personal communication 2002)

Gartrell continues this discussion in *Guidance Matters*. "No other educational practice prepares children for citizenship in a democracy like class meetings. If done well, they tell children 'My ideas matter' and 'I'm glad I belong to this group.' What a positive message to give to a child! What a positive way for educators to affirm the democratic ideal that our society is still striving to attain!" (2006, 3).

He also states "class meetings sustain encouraging classrooms. They are vital to developmentally appropriate early childhood education. . . we cannot start them too early" (2006, 3).

Bredekamp and Copple, editors of *Developmentally Appropriate Practice in Early Childhood Programs,* designated class meetings as a strategy "to help build a sense of the group as a democratic community" (1997, 162). In 2009, Copple and Bredekamp noted that, as a part of communication and language use, it is important for teachers to "engage individual children and groups in real conversations about their experiences" (225).

In *A Guidance Approach for the Encouraging Classroom,* Gartell says,

> Class meetings, then, become a primary method for teaching democratic life skills. Each time a meeting occurs, children are reminded the classroom is a community that includes each one of them as well as each adult. Just as learning centers do for developmentally appropriate practice, class meetings help to define the encouraging classroom. (2014, 253)

Learning to Give Acknowledgments

During the first weeks, meetings may be somewhat limited in their scope. Beginning with the introduction of acknowledgments, teachers start creating trust, positive talk, and sharing. Observing students developing the ability to give acknowledgments presents an opportunity to move forward with problem solving. This happens slowly over the early weeks, or even months, of introducing class meetings, and it can take young children a while to become active participants in the proceedings.

After opening a meeting with a group activity, the teacher can begin by modeling an acknowledgment; for example, he might say, "I would like to acknowledge Aaron for putting the scissors back where they belong this morning." He can then encourage Aaron to thank him (the teacher) for the acknowledgment.

Because *acknowledge* is a difficult and unfamiliar word for many preschoolers, the teacher may want to model thanking individuals as well as acknowledging them. He might say, "I would like to thank our coteacher Sra. Naranjo for reading that story to us in Spanish" or "I would like to thank Chen and Cameron for being

Recording Kind Acts

"Children, in our class we are going to watch for kind and helpful things that people do for one another. Before our meeting, I saw Nicholas help Kai find the right puzzle piece, and I wrote down Nicholas's kind act on this pad of paper in my pocket. I am sure that I will be able to write down many kind acts this morning. Then I will read them aloud in our class meeting before we go to lunch."

On the first day of school, Phyllis Whitin begins teaching her new kindergartners to show consideration, kindness, and respect and to notice when others demonstrate these qualities. She says, "Even in these first hours I want to establish the expectation that we are a community, so all the children can feel safe and respected and have their talents recognized and used by the group" (2001, 18). Whitin tries to find a kind act by every child within a few days. She is especially sure to mention the positive acts of children with potential behavior problems, to help prevent them from feeling unwanted or not valued by the group.

By the end of September, the children themselves are ready to record acts of kindness. Whitin and the children talk about ways to record: writing names, asking their friends to write their own names, drawing pictures, copying signs, and "doing the best you can" (using invented spellings). These small notes go into the Kindness Jar. Before lunch the children assemble in a circle on the rug, and the teacher opens the jar and hands the various authors their slips of paper to read to the class.

Over time the children's reports evolve. Kayla writes, "I was at the sand table. I turned around and peeked over in blocks, and Michael and Furman and Lee were playing nice." Such observations indicate that children are beginning to think beyond themselves and about the general welfare of the class. The notes acknowledging others' kindness help inspire a spirit of collaboration and mutual recognition.

By midyear kindergartners adapt the kindness notes to recognize instances of conflict resolution. Whitin writes, "Throughout the year my teacher assistant and I teach the children conflict management strategies. We review their problem-solving experiences at meeting time, and soon these events become kindness reports."

As the year goes on, the children use kindness notes to describe collaborative investigations in the science and math centers or complex games of dramatic play. They redefine kind acts to include sharing ideas and enjoying each other's company. The class has become a community.

Adapted, by permission, from P. Whitin, "Kindness in a Jar," *Young Children* 56 (September 2001): 18–22.

ready to start our meeting," and follow up by asking the class, "Does anyone have someone you would like to thank or acknowledge?"

The children may need a bit of time to think of an acknowledgment. If they still do not offer an acknowledgment, it is time to move on to a closing activity, saying, for example, "Okay, then, it's time to close the meeting. Tomorrow we'll hold another class meeting. In the meantime, let's try to notice positive actions or things someone else has done that make you feel good."

Most children do not naturally remember small acts of consideration or generosity during their busy days. Recognizing and noting such acts is not an innate behavior; it is a social skill that must be learned. When we teachers observe a thoughtful gesture or act of sharing in the course of the day, we make a point of acknowledging it on the spot: "Manny, I see that you are dividing

Learning to Use I-Feel Statements

Along with acknowledgments, early class meetings can include guiding and teaching children to use I-feel statements as a means to avoid accusation and threat. When the speaker uses this type of statement, she takes responsibility for her feelings rather than blaming another. For example, "You hurt me on the playground" can be restated, "I feel sad when you hurt me." Because the latter avoids accusation, the person addressed feels less threatened and may be more willing to listen. Teachers can take advantage of teachable moments during the day, when a problem arises and the accusations begin flying, to prompt children to use this phrasing.

When you intervene in a conflict, help the children involved to calm down, through breathing exercises or a friendly reminder, then encourage them to use I-feel statements: "Mitchell, use your words to share, not your hands. Let Luz know you feel angry when she grabs the truck you are playing with. And that you want her to stop doing that."

Role-playing is an excellent way to teach communication and social skills in class meetings. You and the children can brainstorm stressful scenarios that children their age might typically experience in the program or school setting, in the neighborhood, and at home. Then ask for volunteers to role-play these situations using I-feel statements.

When the children have mastered I-feel statements, you can extend their problem-solving skills by having them add, "Next time, will you please [show some respect, be more careful, ask me if it's okay, and so on]?"

the crackers with Bernard and Jelani so that each child gets the same amount. Thank you for sharing the crackers this way."

Acknowledgments can also take place outside class meetings—on the playground, in activity centers, and during small-group work. Teachers model acknowledgments and encourage children to follow suit. With reminders from adults and with practice, children begin to develop the disposition to notice and comment on others' constructive acts. (In "Recording Kind Acts" on p. 39, a teacher introduces a strategy to help children note one another's kindness and is pleasantly surprised by its overwhelming success in bringing the children together.)

Giving acknowledgments in class meetings reinforces this disposition. Acknowledgments make children more aware of the many opportunities to help, work with, or reach out to one another, and the positive feedback children receive makes them more likely to act on such opportunities again. What begins for children as an exercise in observation develops eventually into a climate of caring and community.

Sometimes older children who have not participated in class meetings may feel uncomfortable during the acknowledgments part of the meeting. Some may laugh or say they cannot think of anything good to say. However, as you continue to hold meetings, children learn to look forward to this part. Acknowledgments make the giver and the receiver feel good. In addition to significantly affecting the classroom climate, they build children's self-esteem. One child in our class said, "I like acknowledgments because they make me feel good inside."

When young children have not yet begun to offer contributions to the meeting, the teacher can draw them in by posing questions or using prompts: "Taylor, I noticed you and Suki playing with the soccer ball on the playground . . ." or "Alexandra, I noticed that Tanya pushed you on the swing . . ." Such statements can be followed by questions: Did you enjoy having Tanya push you on the swing? Did you go really high? Did you push Tanya on the swing?

Similarly, when young children begin to come forward with acknowledgments, the teacher can engage them in brief conversations, eliciting the details of their interactions with other children. For example, if a preschool child says, "Alem, thank you for being my friend," the teacher can ask questions: What were you doing together? Did you take turns? Did you laugh? Was it fun? What makes someone a friend?

Another focus for initial class meetings is talking about and practicing I-feel statements. (See "Learning to Use I-Feel Statements" on p. 40.) Learning to express negative emotions using I-feel statements begins when teachers intervene in conflicts in the classroom or on the playground. However, adopting this form of expression takes time. As conflicts occur, teachers can model and encourage children to use I-feel statements whenever possible. For example, the teacher might ask, "How did you feel when Jody said he didn't want to play with you?" With young children, the teacher may even provide the first two words by saying "I feel . . . " and then asking, "How do you feel?" The child may respond using an I-feel statement like, "I felt sad when he didn't want to play with me."

When most of the children seem to have mastered acknowledgments and I-feel statements, it is time to introduce a new element into class meetings: group problem solving.

Smart Moves

Hannaford addresses brain research in her book *Smart Moves: Why Learning Is Not All in Your Head* that establishes the limbic system as an "emotional filter." Hannaford shares that "the limbic system has links with the neocortex allowing for emotional cognitive processing" (1995, 59.) She further states that the amygdala has links to brain areas involved in cognitive processing as well as those involved in bodily states related to the whole gamut of emotions from powerful reactions of grief or pain to pleasure and joy. After sharing this exercise with kindergartners, many chose to do this on their own to help them stay calm and focus on listening during story time or when they wanted a moment to calm down. Children became more aware of time as they realized how long two minutes can seem. Hannaford writes that "as a counselor, I had a two-minute rule. When students (ages 5 to 15) were sent to me for being disruptive in the classroom or following a playground fight they had to sit in "hook-ups" for two minutes before we talked." She extends this further stating that "following the two minutes they were able to see both their own and each others' point of view more clearly" (p. 134).

Here is a description of Hannaford's hook-up:

> Hook-ups are done first by crossing one ankle over the other—whichever feels most comfortable. The hands are then crossed, clasped and inverted. To do this, stretch your arms out in front of you, with the back of the hands together and the thumbs pointing down. Now lift one hand over the other, palms facing down and interlock the fingers. Then roll the locked hands straight down and in toward the body so they eventually rest on the chest with the elbows down. While in this position rest the tongue on the roof of the mouth behind the teeth. (p. 133)

This exercise creates an intricate action crossing over the midline that "activates the sensory and motor cortices of each hemisphere of the cerebrum." After reading this information, I reminded myself to provide children in highly emotional states an opportunity to calm down. After sharing this exercise with kindergartners, many chose to do this on their own to help them stay calm and focus on listening during story time or when they wanted a moment to calm down. Children became more aware of time as they realized how long two minutes can seem.

Hannaford's "Hook-up" exercise is an invaluable tool for helping children relax and refocus, and it provides time for the teacher to relax when practiced this at the beginning or ending of the class meetings.

There is recent research on the neurobiology of emotional intelligence using our brain to stay cool under pressure. Bruno adds that "we have nerve cells called mirror neurons that allow us, without thinking, to mimic the feelings and movements of people around us" (2011, 23). Geake (2009) also refers to this mirror neuron system in the context of storytelling and enabling mental social simulation.

Introducing Problem Solving

Just as teachers teach acknowledgments and I-feel statements in authentic situations, so they introduce the language and strategies of problem solving while helping children resolve conflicts when they occur. Mindful that she is modeling problem-solving techniques, the teacher calmly approaches a conflict between children and helps the children calm down. Some children have difficulty calming down quickly. In these cases, I have found taking a few minutes of time to provide exercises that help them relax and gain composure make it easier to engage in the problem-solving process. (See "Smart Moves," exercises for calming, on p. 43.)

Next, the teacher listens to each child's view without expressing judgment or opinion and validates each child's feelings. After gathering the information, the teacher restates the problem and asks the children to think of solutions that might work

Empathy

DeVries and Zan (1994) extend the work of Piaget ([1954] 1981) in favor of the "sociomoral atmosphere" in classrooms. They maintain that "all interactions between and among children and their caregivers/educators have an impact on children's social and moral experience and development" (1994,1). In a related approach, Gardner (1983, 1993, 1999) identified intelligences or ways in which people learn or acquire knowledge in his Multiple Intelligences theory. Of particular interest are Gardner's (1999) interpersonal and intrapersonal intelligences: "Interpersonal intelligence denotes a person's capacity to understand the intentions, motivations, and desire of other people and consequently, to work effectively with others" (43). Gardner also revealed that although intrapersonal intelligence relates to the "understanding of oneself" (1999, 43) and the appreciation of this information in regulating one's own life, it also leads us to a path of self-inquiry in which the self develops out of interactions with the environment and significant others.

Gardner has considered adding a moral intelligence to his theory of Multiple Intelligences. He states, "Many individuals believe that human beings have a moral capacity that is present from birth and that morality follows a predictable trajectory through maturity" (2006, 28). Goleman extended his emotional intelligence theory to include social intelligence, which he defines as the interconnection of "being intelligent not just about relationships but also in them" (2006, 11). Goleman continued his argument stating, "Schools themselves are a very recent artifact of civilization. The more powerful force in the brain's architecture is arguably the need to navigate the social world, for them. She asks bystanders for their ideas as well. When the children with the problem decide on a solution they are comfortable with, they say, "Our problem is solved." This type of statement provides a way of expressing closure to the situation. There are other ways to demonstrate this closure such as asking how the children feel about their efforts in resolving their dilemma or asking if they would be willing to share how their day went after they had an opportunity to solve a problem. In this way children become familiar with the concepts and vocabulary of problem solving before the teacher introduces it in class meetings.

Books can be an effective way to interject conflict resolution into the class meeting agenda. When a problem crops up, the teacher can select a children's book in which the characters have a similar problem and work out a solution. This technique takes planning and forethought. The teacher needs to be thoroughly

not the need to get As" (2006, 334). Goleman further suggested that we look at social intelligence as the umbrella over general intelligence (Vance 2009).

There may be a relationship between the group dynamics of class meetings and the social and moral capacities of young children. Consider the following example. After we gathered together for a class meeting, I noticed that Byron was visibly upset. I called on Byron to talk and he said, "I want to give an acknowledgment." I responded with the probing question, "How can I help you?" He replied, "I feel mean." Because I thought that Byron said, "I want an acknowledgment," I turned to the class meeting group and asked if anyone in the class meeting circle would like to give Byron an acknowledgment. There was a distinct pause from the children. Finally, one child, Marcos, raised his hand. Marcos said, "I want to acknowledge Byron for playing with me." Byron retorted in a strong, angry voice. "He did not!" I returned to Marcos and said, "Byron does not seem to remember playing with you. Are you sure you did this?" Marcos shook his head side to side as if to say, "No." I then asked, "Did you want to give him (Byron) an acknowledgment to make him feel better?" Marcos said, "Yes." What was profound to me was that after Byron realized Marcos's intention was to try and make him feel better, Byron's behavior changed, and he calmed down. We were able to proceed with the remainder of this class meeting. At subsequent class meetings, Byron came voluntarily. He was ready to participate, and there was no evidence of Byron projecting anger within the class meeting circle. This example highlights a young child (Marcos) expressing empathy and using abstract, cognitive, and interpersonal skills to support making moral decisions and the impact on his peer.

familiar with the book's content (Jalongo 1986). This is especially important when books deal with feelings, attitudes, beliefs, and values.

Jalongo suggests that the teacher comment on why she has chosen to read this particular book—that is, let the children know that a certain classroom incident or problem made her think about sharing the book with them—and that the teacher pose questions as she reads: "Questions that encourage children to analyze the behavior of story characters, make inferences about emotional reactions, apply information to their own experience, and synthesize techniques for coping with crises are all appropriate" (1986, 46). Short highlights the importance of children's inquiry within the classroom curriculum. Short also shares the significance of "multiple literacies, where various ways of knowing and being are encouraged and enhanced" (Short & Harste 1996, 53).

Abramson extends on the work of Short by suggesting "when undertaken by a small group of learners, co-inquiry stimulates different ideas and perspectives. As a result, participants acquire knowledge, skills, dispositions, and values" (2012, 150).

Finally the teacher summarizes the story, rephrases the basic concepts, and responds to children's questions, reinforcing ideas and points relevant to the classroom conflict at issue.

Or the teacher might read a familiar story such as *Goldilocks and the Three Bears* and ask for volunteers to act it out. Role-playing can help children better understand a storybook character's motives and feelings. I often create generic problems and talk with some volunteers prior to the meeting about acting out this dilemma. For example, I may ask, What suggestions do you have to help Goldilocks to be safe on the way to her grandmother's house? Is it a good idea to tell a stranger where you are going?

Taylor et al. (2013, 80) discuss the familiar role-playing games of "house" and "doctor." These games open opportunities for discussion within the class meeting. For example, "I noticed you were playing house today in the home center. Did you have any problems?" If the child says yes, ask, "What did you do?" If the child says no, ask, "How did you keep from having a problem?" or "How did you make it fun and get along?" (Children can also role-play the questions listed in "What If We Don't Have a Problem?" on p. 30). By switching roles, children can be encouraged to see a problem from more than one point of view. Through role play children can begin to grasp social skills like empathy and perspective-taking that are crucial to problem solving. "Children's Books for Building Conflict Resolution Skills" (on pp. 48–49), a brief annotated list of books that lend themselves to children's group discussions about problem solving, appears at the end of this chapter.

To avoid focusing negative attention on a child, when the teacher introduces the first classroom problems to be resolved in class meeting, she should do so in general terms without mentioning names: "Yesterday at the water table there was some arguing and grabbing, and a lot of water spilled on the floor and on people's shoes and socks. I wonder what we can do to keep this from occurring again at the water table? Does anyone have an idea?" The teacher then guides the discussion, prompting the children by modeling the use of the problem-solving language they use to determine solutions to individual conflicts. With a problem posed this way, children are less likely to feel defensive, and the issue becomes a general one requiring the group's involvement (Kriedler & Whittall 1999). Bullard and Bullock expand on this by pointing out that "the group dialogue can also create a synergy, producing an effect that is greater than the sum of any one individual's knowledge or experience" (2004, 40).

After the children tackle a few such disputes, and when the teacher senses that they are ready, she can begin to have children introduce individual conflicts in class meeting. On the playground she might say, "Bart, I see that you and Renee are having trouble taking turns on the red trike. I've noticed other people having the same problem. That is a very popular tricycle. Would you and Renee agree to explain your problem in class meeting today? Perhaps the entire class can do some thinking and come up with ways to share the trike." Teachers will be amazed at how willingly children set aside their disagreements and get on with the business of playing and learning when they know the problem will be cleared up later in class meeting. The teacher may also present this as a form of redirection and invite the children involved in the problem to try and think of some ways that might work to share with the other children. This changes the focus and often children

Children's Books for Building Conflict Resolution Skills

Aardema, Verna. *Why Mosquitoes Buzz in People's Ears: A West African Tale.* An excellent story about the consequences of telling a lie.

Allard, Henry. *Miss Nelson Is Missing.* An amusing tale about a teacher who was disliked by her students, then ultimately about the importance of respect.

Bang, Molly. When Sophie Gets Angry—*Really, Really Angry.* A powerful story that shows that strong feelings, like anger, can be managed.

Bruchac, Joseph. *The First Strawberries: A Cherokee Story.* This traditional tale provides a useful lesson about hurt and forgiveness.

Curtis, Jamie Lee. *It's Hard to Be Five: Learning How to Work My Control Panel.* An amusing book about self-control.

DePaola, Tomie. *The Knight and the Dragon.* Use this amusing story about a knight and a dragon to talk about how to turn competition into collaboration, to find peaceful solutions.

Derolf, Sharon and Letzig, Michael. *The Crayon Box That Talked.* A delightful story that delivers the powerful message about the importance of getting along and being accepting of diversity.

Guback, Georgia. *Luka's Quilt.* Luka and her grandmother resolve a conflict they have over the quilt her grandmother made. This story is excellent for discussing win-win solutions.

Havill, Juanita. *Jamaica and Brianna.* Two friends are jealous and say hurtful things to each other. Good for discussions about different points of view and putdowns.

Henkes, Kevin. *Chrysanthemum.* This book is about being the victim of teasing, but it is also about the importance of the love and support of family.

Hoffman, Mary. *Amazing Grace.* Grace wants to play the role of Peter Pan in the school play. This story of following one's dreams regardless of the barriers is a good book to talk about problem solving and counteracting bias.

Hutchins, Pat. *The Doorbell Rang.* A cumulative tale that explores the challenge of sharing.

Katz, Karen. *The Colors of Us.* A book that celebrates our differences and our similarities.

Lionni, Leo. *Six Crows.* An updated telling of a fable shows the value of communication. Good for focusing on communicating feelings and needs.

Lionni, Leo. *Swimmy.* A small fish shows the other fish the power of cooperation. This book can also be used to talk about conflict resolution.

Marsden, Carolyn. *The Gold-Threaded Dress.* This is a story about young Thai-American girl succumbing to peer pressure at school. A good book for discussions about peer pressure, bullying, and cultural awareness.

Mitchell, Lori. *Different Just Like Me.* A sweet story that celebrates the similarities and differences among people.

O'Neill, Alexis. *The Recess Queen.* Mean Jean is the recess queen until a new girl, Katie Sue, arrives one day. A good book to talk about bullying and conflict resolution.

Otoshi, Kathryn. *One.* A counting book that is really about bullying, getting along, and accepting differences.

Pfister, Marcus. *The Rainbow Fish.* A visually appealing book about friendship and sharing.

Rosen, Michael. *This Is Our House.* This amusing book that shows how to turn exclusiveness into inclusiveness is good for working on prejudices and anti-bias, conflicts over playmates, and sharing play materials.

Rosenthal, Amy Krouse. *One Smart Cooke: Bite-Size Lesson for the School Years and Beyond.* This book uses cookie-related words to explain important concepts like contribute, empathy, and integrity.

Scieszka, Jon. *The True Story of the Three Little Pigs by A. Wolf.* The popular fairy tale told from the point of view of the Big Bad Wolf. Excellent for working on perspective taking.

Seuss, Dr. *The Sneeches and Other Stories.* Three good stories about conflict. "The Sneeches" is especially good for talking about anti-bias issues. "The Zax" is good for talking about lose-lose solutions to conflicts.

Silverman, Erica. *Don't Fidget a Feather.* Duck and Gander always compete over who's best. This book about friendship and competition is excellent for discussing win-lose, lose-lose, and win-win solutions, as well as competitive (winner-loser) games.

Spelman, Cornela Maude. *When I Feel Angry.* A young rabbit gets angry, but learns how to deal with her anger. Excellent for a discussion about how to behave when angry.

Zolotow, Charlotte. *The Hating Book.* A little girl learns the value of communication and friendship. Good for talking about strong emotions and for focusing on relationships and communication skills.

Zolotow, Charlotte. *The Quarreling Book.* This simple book about a family that quarrels is excellent for a discussion about emotions and how our feelings can be passed along to others.

Parts of this list are adapted, by permission, from N. Carlsson-Paige & D.E. Levin, *Before Push Comes to Shove: Building Conflict Resolution Skills With Children* (St. Paul, MN: Redleaf, 1998), 87–89.

Also, special thanks for Alyssa Haymen for her assistance with compiling part of this list.

are delighted to share how they were able to reach a solution before the meeting.

Glasser says,

> If children learn to participate in a problem-solving group when they enter school and continue to do so with a variety of teachers throughout the six years of elementary school, they learn that the world is not a mysterious and sometimes hostile and frightening place where they have little control over what happens to them. They learn that, although the world may be difficult and that it may at times appear hostile and mysterious, they can use their brains individually and as a group to solve the problems of living in their school world. (1969, 123)

I have found such benefits can begin with toddlers, preschoolers, and kindergartners.

Two Examples of Problem Solving in Class Meetings

The Trap Problem

When the new children's kitchen furniture arrived for the dramatic play area, right away the children were anxious to play with it. Marilina crawled inside to investigate the bottom shelf under the small kitchen sink. Some classmates got together and closed the cupboard doors. Then they put a stick through the handle door handles, locking her inside. Marilina realized that she was trapped and unable to get out. She pushed her back against the cupboard doors and cried out for help. The teacher quickly removed the stick and opened the cabinet doors. The next day during our class meeting, Marilina shared what happened with the children.

Marilina: I was very sad when the boys locked me inside.

Teacher: Boys, do you remember when Marilina was trapped inside the play kitchen yesterday?

Boys: Yes.

Teacher: Marilina, what would you like to tell the children?

Marilina: Please don't do that again.

Teacher: Boys are you willing not to do that again?

Boys: Yes.

Teacher: Would you like to shake hands?

Marilina: Yes, we can hold hands.

Teacher: Boys, are you willing to hold hands with Marilina and let her know what you will do next time?

Boys: We won't do that again.

This class meeting exemplifies the importance of supporting the development of classroom communication skills. Utilizing the class meeting approach, the children and teacher co-constructed an awareness of how their behavior affects others. Once Marilina told the boys that she was sad and asked them not to do this again, they became aware that what had happened was not safe and agreed to be more respectful in the future. In the class meeting, Marilina felt the accomplishment of using her words to resolve her problem. This reinforced the notion that children often do not require punitive measures against each other to achieve resolutions. It is important to note that afterward the teacher was proactive by removing one of the cabinet handles to avoid this type of incident from reoccurring and further ensure student safety within the classroom.

The Kicking Problem

The topic for this class meeting was introduced by the teacher as a result of student observations and interactions.

Teacher: Last week, I noticed something happening on the playground during outdoor time. There was a kicking problem. What can we do if someone is kicking us?

Ashley: Say "stop" or "please stop." (*Ashley put the flat palm of her hand straight out in front of her, like she was directing traffic.*)

Teacher: Okay. Do we tell them to stop in a soft voice or do we use a strong voice?

Children: Strong voice.

Emily: The only way is by being nice to people.

Ryan: Say "Stop kicking me, please."

Teacher: You can also say "Please show me respect." What other way could you solve the kicking problem?

Jacob: Go away from them.

Skyler: People follow you and you say "Stop" and they still follow you.

Esteven: If somebody follows you, you ignore them and I go up the slide (to get away from them.)

Teacher: What about getting more friends to join you?

Juliette: Make friends.

Teacher: Let's see. Here are some of the things that you have suggested in our class meeting today that you can do if you have a kicking problem.

1. Say "Please stop," "Stop kicking me please," or "Show me respect."

2. You can move away from the person that is kicking.

3. You can ignore them (the person that is kicking) and go to the slide or some other safe place.

Teacher: We have some ideas on how to solve a kicking problem. I want to thank all of you for coming together in our class meeting and sharing ways to make school a safe place. You are welcome to bring this topic up at another class meeting if you need other strategies or ways to deal with the kicking problem.

●　　●　　●　　●

After looking closely at acknowledgments and problem solving, the key components of class meetings, and how to introduce them to children, the next chapter focuses on how to vary or adapt class meetings.

5

Class Meeting Variations and Adaptations

This chapter focuses on several types of class meetings and problem-solving contexts that vary in one way or another from the basic class meeting. The first focuses on working with children who are emergent English-language learners or dual language learners (DLLs). Next, the chapter addresses occasions when problem solving takes place with only the children directly involved in an incident or problem rather than with the whole class—a mini meeting. Another variation is to utilize levity and laughter as a way of building a classroom community.

Finally, Sylvia Chard discusses the Project Approach and class meetings. While these group meetings differ from the meetings described earlier (which had a focus on solving children's interpersonal problems), Chard's discussion shows how in collaborative work children's problem solving and thinking together strengthen the skills used in class meetings and vice versa.

Class Meetings With Dual Language Learners

In order to support children's understanding, vocabulary development, and appreciation of cultural diversity, it is important to provide scaffolding during the meetings. With dual language learners, a teacher may observe the child and check back to make sure she understands and to see if she has any questions. If there is another child, parent, or teaching assistant who speaks the home language, I ask him to sit next to the child and help translate. I also try to sit close to any child who may need additional assistance. In today's classrooms, many children need this support. Having daily class meetings provides the teacher with opportunities to sit next to different children throughout the week.

Children enjoy knowing that class meetings are a wonderful way to learn new language skills. If a child is willing, the class meeting becomes a way to share words from his home language with his classmates and increase awareness of other cultures. This provides a comfortable, meaningful environment in which children can build oral language skills using their "funds of knowledge" to support and create community interconnectedness (Moll & Whitmore 1993). Ethnographic research supports the importance of teachers incorporating into the curriculum students' prior social and learning experiences derived from their home, family, and culture (Gonzalez, Moll, & Amanti 2005).

In my experience, it is important to involve parents in their child's learning experience by modeling use of the home language, pattern language, and frequently used words. I also use role-playing with parents to teach them the components of the class meeting (specifically acknowledgments and problem-solving questions). Parents can then encourage their child at home, sharing the class meeting vocabulary and procedures. During the class meetings, on occasion DLLs speak or code switch, interchanging words from their home language and English. In these instances, the teacher can extend oral language development by modeling appropriate responses.

If two children in a class meeting discussion speak the same first language, it is easy for them to begin talking to each other. In this case, it is helpful to give an occasional update to the children who are not fluent in the language the children are using. Appointing other children to translate is an ideal way to involve more children in the meeting.

Recognizing the language dynamics during class meeting can result in benefits for home and second language acquisition. The important point is that children are more likely to learn a language when they are highly motivated to use it. When two children have a problem, the need to communicate their feelings to one another is powerful.

Mini Meetings: Solving Problems in Small Groups

Not every topic is appropriate for class meeting. Some issues are likely to cause children embarrassment. Others can be dealt with right when they occur. For any of several reasons, the teacher may decide that a mini meeting rather than a class meeting is the way to go. When using mini meetings, as with larger class meetings, it is important for the children themselves to take ownership of the problem-solving process (McClurg 1998). For mini meetings, the components of the class meeting (opening, acknowledgments, problem solving, and closing) may be adjusted to address the problem at hand quickly, followed by a short closing, asking the children involved if their problem has been solved.

It may be the child's personality or the nature of the problem, or both, that makes a smaller meeting preferable in a particular instance. Yvette, for example, is a quiet child who is more
comfortable talking in small groups than in whole-class meetings.
Consequently, during class meetings she seldom speaks out if she
has a problem.

One day Yvette told me she had a problem with three girls
who were ignoring her during lunch. I thanked her for taking the
initiative to solve the problem. I asked her if she wanted to discuss
this issue during a class meeting. She opted instead for a mini meeting with the three girls and they successfully resolved the issue.

Yvette continued using mini meetings as a method of addressing problems. Although she never discussed a problem in
a large class meeting, she began talking more to the teachers
because of her growing confidence and sense of trust from the
success of the mini-meeting alternative.

Some teachers may be reluctant to use class meetings,
fearing that an issue will unexpectedly be introduced that embar-
rasses a child or is inappropriate for group discussion. Certainly
sensitive issues may come up in class meetings from time to
time—issues related to sexual conduct, personal hygiene, or racism, for example. Or a child from an abusive home may bring up
matters that require the attention of the school counselor or a
decision about notifying social services or the authorities.

If such a topic is broached in a class meeting, the teacher can
tactfully head off the discussion by requesting time to gather more
information, or to ask school experts, such as the counselor or
social worker; opting to address the subject with the child in private; or suggesting that the children involved meet later with her
in a mini meeting. On occasion we must admit that we do not have
all the answers to all questions. What is important is that children
learn their problems can be addressed and that a viable problem
solving strategy is to ask others for further information.

Laughter Meetings

According to Wubbolding, children are able to learn when they
are happy, and they are happy when they have healthy interpersonal relationships (2007). Klein extends this by saying that

Bullying

The roots of a bully's behavior are found in early childhood, when patterns of social interaction are formed. A need for power, control, or attention is often the motivation for bullying behavior. An example of a child trying to fulfill this need is when he or she uses the familiar, simple, songlike chant, "Nanny, nanny, pooh, pooh, you can't come to my birthday party!," as a way to embarrass or exclude another child. Coloroso (2003) calls this the bullying play or the script that a bully uses to express contempt for another, generating a "powerful feeling of dislike for somebody considered worthless, inferior or undeserving of respect" (p. 20). She states that "bullying is arrogance in action" (2003, 21). In the scenario with the songlike chant, the child singing the taunting song is the *bully*. The child being sung to, the target of contempt, is the *bullied*. Others observing this situation are *bystanders*. Each one has a role in this drama and each must receive additional guidance and support to eliminate the negative behavior. "These terms are not meant to permanently label children but rather provide a way to identify certain roles and characteristics" (Coloroso 2003, 4). As an early childhood professional, I have observed this scenario many times and over the years developed a way of responding that seemed to work.

Sometimes the bully and bullied need the help of others to establish that the bullying behavior actually occurred. For example, when talking to the child who was doing the bullying, you may sense that he is fearful of confessing or stating his involvement in the problem. He may say no when asked if he remembers the situation. This is a good time to invite the bystanders to share further information. These testimonials provide more details and confirmation, or verification, of the situation. I have found that when a child who has demonstrated bullying behavior becomes aware that others observed her actions, it defuses her ability to deny participation in the drama. Other times, bystanders are unable to give information that either confirms or denies the actions. In such cases, we might talk about how we will have to be more observant as we go forward. Class meetings or mini meetings are effective forums for addressing less severe types of bullying, like the example above.

humor is a tool that helps children establish meaningful, mutually respectful relationships with peers and adults. When children share humor with others, they experience a sense of connection, value, and group identity" (Klein 2003, 4). Lyon (2006) tells us that " . . . humour is a skill that can be trained." Interestingly, Gardner also states in 2006 that he had considered adding humor as another one of his multiple intelligences (2006, 27).

Another variation of the class meeting is to simply come together to laugh, play, de-stress, and strengthen the classroom community. When introducing Laughter Meetings, I often ask children, "Would you like to laugh with me?" It is amazing to see the looks on their faces. Encouraging children to laugh together is not common in the school routine, due to the pressures of schedules and curriculum. Unfortunately, sometimes others interpret levity in the classroom as a teacher's lack of control. Asking children to laugh together provides a refreshing breather in the daily routine. As the children come together in a circle, I teach several transition activities that help bring them back together.

- The first transition is clapping to the right, then the left, then reaching up above the head saying "Very good, very good, yeah."

- The next is to reach up above the head saying "Yeah."

- The third transition is clapping to the right to a 1, 2 rhythm saying "Ho, Ho," then moving the hands to the left side clapping to a 1, 2, 3 rhythm saying "Ha, Ha, Ha."

Any of these transitions are great ways to bring the group focus back together. After the children have practiced the transitions it is time to introduce some laughter exercises to motivate their laughter. Children have little problem joining in on the fun.

- One laughter exercise is Cell Phone Laughter. Children pretend that someone funny is on the other end of an imaginary phone. They are invited to move around and share their cell phone with other classmates while continuing to laugh. This is followed by one of the transitions.

- Another fun activity is to play Red Light, Green Light. Two children are asked to be helpers. One is assigned to say "green light." The other will say "red light." We start out by telling the children to pretend they are imaginary laughing cars. When they hear "green light," they start driving their car carefully around the room saying, "Ahahahahhaha." When they hear "red light," they can step on the brake and laugh loudly. The more the two children say "green light" and "red light," the more laughing will occur.

To bring the children back together, we chant and clap "Ho, Ho, Ha, Ha, Ha" to the 1, 2, 1, 2, 3 rhythm. (Special thanks to Dr. Madan Kataria for these laughter exercises [Kataria 2011].)

Class Meetings

Using Laughter to Create a Joyful Classroom Community

A fellow preschool teacher, Kathy Janssen, shared this story about her classroom of 4- and 5-year-olds using laughter exercises. One child spoke only Japanese with his mother, who accompanied and supported him during his first weeks at the school. He spoke very little English. In fact, he could only say *hello* and *good-bye*. This child appeared nervous and shy, seeking constant one-to-one adult attention with limited interactions with the other children.

Soon, he started joining in during class meetings. Kathy noticed that he especially enjoyed the meetings that focused on using laughter exercises. She observed him many times using the cell phone laughter exercise. This is when the children put one hand up close to an ear and laugh into an imaginary cell phone. Kathy remembers observing him when this activity was first introduced to the class. His broad smile conveyed his enjoyment and understanding. Then, he started using this as a way to communicate with his classmates. He would start laughing into his pretend phone and then hand it to another child who would laugh back with him. Before long, he felt safe enough to start adding a few English words into his play phone, such as *yes, no, you,* and *phone.* As he continued to laugh using the cell phone, he appeared more and more comfortable. Before long, he began incorporating even more English vocabulary words. This proved to be a safe way for him to socialize with the other children.

Within a few weeks, Kathy noticed that schoolmates started playing with him and he was interacting with the other children more often and with more ease. Kathy also shared how important she felt it was to let this child take the time to be quiet and when he was ready, move forward with his language development.

Class Meetings and the Project Approach

Many teachers regularly offer opportunities for children to make choices and take ownership of tasks. Class meetings can help children attain developmentally appropriate levels of achievement in individualized work and provide a forum for collaborative planning as well. During class meetings, teachers can present task alternatives and help children make appropriate choices.

The project approach is one framework that works especially well with class meetings. As described in *Engaging Children's Minds: The Project Approach* (Katz, Chard, & Kogan forthcoming), projects

---

Note: Sylvia C. Chard, PhD, a leading expert on the project approach, wrote and contributed to the section titled "Class Meetings and the Project Approach" in this chapter. Sylvia is a Professor Emeritus of Early Childhood Education at the University of Alberta in Edmonton, Canada.

are in-depth studies of topics or themes such as bicycles, birds, or the desert, and the project approach enables children to make choices and work independently while exploring those studies. During project work, children choose from among alternatives, develop individual interests, and undertake independent investigations responsibly. Children can also develop strategies for solving problems on their own or with friends, and many projects are collaborative studies in which the children in the class take part.

Project work is a beneficial but challenging teaching strategy, and class meetings can address these challenges through increased communication. When teachers share the planning of project work with the class, children feel ownership in the way projects develop. Throughout the study, class meetings can be used as a venue for children to share plans, interesting features of their work, and ideas for new directions.

As they learn to appreciate the work of their classmates, children are better able to evaluate their own efforts as well. Finally, children can celebrate the conclusion of a project by using class meetings to plan a culminating event or exhibition of learning.

Class meetings are an excellent time to introduce a topic of study. During the first phase of the project (about a week in duration), the class can discuss relevant personal experiences and

Components of a Project-Oriented Class Meeting

When doing project work during class meetings, the following components are particularly helpful:

Sharing (telling others about what you are doing, listening to what others tell you about what they are doing) interests, expertise, achievements, concerns, intentions

Problem solving (recognizing when there is a problem that can be solved appropriately by class meetings), problem stating, seeking solutions

Acknowledging (appreciating individual children who have facilitated other children's work) help given, ideas, practical help obtaining material, appreciation by other children

Modeling (the appropriate, the optimum) dispositions that support learning by helping children solve problems independently, seek advice from other children and/or the teacher, become deeply involved in work, concentrate, and be persistent

reflect on what they already know about the topic. Teachers and children can brainstorm questions they would like to investigate and ways of documenting their experience and knowledge, such as drawing and dramatic play.

The second phase of project work involves fieldwork, conducted either in the classroom through the study of real objects and interviewing experts or by taking the children outside the classroom walls to a local field site. During class meetings, children can share what they have learned from these investigations and remind one another of the various ways of representing what they are learning about the topic.

Once the project is well under way, children often pursue their own individual interests; class meetings enable children to share their unique interests and questions while demonstrating the particular contribution their work is making to the collaborative study as a whole.

Class meetings provide teachers with an opportunity to evaluate and model valuable features of children's work. Sometimes a teacher will comment on original or imaginative ideas in a child's work, while in other instances he will point out the care and attention to detail or a neat and attractive presentation. Particular

Ten Essential Questions in Project Work

In a class project a few essential questions regularly arise. (They are listed here in order of importance.) Class meetings provide a good opportunity for the group to discuss these questions.

1. What aspects of the topic shall we study?
2. What experience do we have of the topic?
3. What questions do we have about the topic?
4. Who might know some of the answers?
5. Where can we go to find out?
6. Which books can help us?
7. What are we each most interested in?
8. How can we represent what we are learning?
9. What are the highlights of the project when it is completed?
10. How can we share what we have learned with others?

All of these questions are of importance to both teachers and children, although teachers may have more expertise in answering some of them. These questions will help teachers and children become more familiar with project work, enabling rich discussions that lead to a greater understanding of the topic at hand. In turn, children will learn to take initiative in their work and to be accountable to the class for their individual contributions to the project.

strengths of children's work can be emphasized for the benefit of the class. Children will often strive to improve their work and be more confident in their efforts when they have appropriate models.

In class meetings children can plan an event at the end of the project for sharing their work with others, including parents, grandparents, and other children. Through collaborative evaluation the children will decide the most important parts of the study to be shared, and how to do so. Perhaps they will perform a skit about an expert they interviewed or show a series of pictures explaining a process they have used. These activities are useful in involving children in reflection and evaluation of the project as a whole.

In addition to the questions that come up regularly during project work (see "Ten Essential Questions in Project Work" on this page), others arising throughout the life of a project can be addressed in class meetings, such as What stories and knowledge do we or our families have to share about our experiences of the topic? Which tasks or activities can we accomplish? What are some of the most interesting fieldwork observations? What are some ways of representing what we've learned? Who will come to share the learning of the class at the end of the study? How will they be invited? Who will write letters of thanks to guests who have helped in the study?

As children address questions like these, they develop a shared understanding of the process of studying a topic in-depth. Reflections and discussions during class meetings help children appreciate their learning community and realize that they have made a personal contribution to a collaborative group effort. They are gaining important skills—not only for the classroom, but also for learning effectively throughout their lives.

The Variations Are Endless

This chapter has examined several variations on the basic class meeting theme: meetings with emergent language learners, mini meetings, using laughter, and working on group projects. Other variations will evolve as individual teachers develop meeting procedures and other problem-solving formats that work best for them and the children in their classes. As in all teaching, plan carefully, and then learn as you go along. The children themselves are always teaching us.

Frequently Asked Questions

6

ere are some of the questions that often arise when talking with other teachers and parents about class meetings,
along with brief responses.

Don't class meetings take valuable time away from teaching?

*Class meetings not only save time by reducing discipline problems
but also accomplish other cognitive and social-emotional goals for
children.*

Rather than wasting learning time, the meetings actually
save time that would be taken up with discipline problems and
interpersonal conflicts. In many instances, problems that would
otherwise interrupt children's learning can be tabled until meeting
time. Once children are used to solving conflicts in class meetings,
they tend to wait and bring up problems at the meeting rather
than require the teacher's immediate attention during classroom
activities.

Knowing their problems will be addressed improves children's ability to concentrate. As children master the problem-
solving strategies used in class meetings, they can apply these
strategies to solve problems on their own. The problem solving

and perspective taking that occur in group meetings strengthen children's use of such skills in other areas of the curriculum and their daily lives.

When a conflict arises, I usually try to help the children involved to resolve it right then and there. Do class meetings have any value *beyond* the benefits of on-the-spot problem solving?

While on-the-spot problem solving with children has an important place, there are times when addressing problems in class meetings is preferable and times when doing both is worthwhile.

Extended conflict resolution right after a problem erupts may or may not be a good idea in a particular instance. The children may be too upset to think clearly. There's also the time that is spent and the likelihood that children's engagement in learning is interrupted. Having the option of class meetings provides time for the children to calm down, time to work on their own to reach a solution, time for the class to come together with the intention of problem solving, and the option of tabling a problem that is likely to take some real working through. Since the children present their problem at a meeting, they take the responsibility and ownership for resolving their problem. Another added benefit of the class meeting is that brainstorming and evaluating possible solutions as a group tend to produce a wider range of ideas and more thoughtful consideration of what might work through collective group thinking. Children often see problems more clearly when they themselves are not directly involved. We all do, in fact. By listening to two or more perspectives on a problem—someone else's problem—the children who are not involved in the original episode learn that a situation can look quite different depending on one's point of view. Even though they may not be involved in the problem, they can participate in helping others resolve their conflicts, a vital step toward building a caring classroom community.

Does the teacher risk losing control of the classroom when he shares authority with the children?

In expressing their opinions in class meetings, children may sometimes become emotional and the discussion heated, but the results are positive.

Some teachers who want to maintain their position of authority in the classroom may object to giving children any control. They are afraid that group problem solving will result in chaos. But in a well-run class meeting, the teacher guides discussion and helps children stay on track and focused on the issues. Reminding the children at the beginning of the meeting that the purpose of the class meeting is to support respectful problem solving helps defuse tensions. The teacher always has the option to postpone the meeting to another time. When teachers follow the basic guidelines presented in this book, class meetings can be orderly and effective. Rather than detract from effective classroom management, the meetings contribute to it.

I worry about sensitive issues coming up in the group situation.

The teacher facilitates group meetings, so she can quickly step in if a problem seems likely to cause a child embarrassment or be inappropriate for class discussion.

Sensitive issues do come up in meetings from time to time—sexual conduct, personal hygiene, or racism, for example. When a child makes a negative remark about someone else's race, gender, or disability, the teacher can often engage the children in an antibias conversation right then (for guidance, see Derman-Sparks & Olsen Edwards 2010; Levin 2013). Alternatively, the teacher may choose to handle a biased remark by engaging the children in a fuller discussion later.

Children may bring up sensitive matters that require the attention of the school counselor or a decision about notifying social services or other authorities. When this happens, the teacher can head off discussion and address the subject with the child in private or suggest that the children involved meet later with her in a mini meeting. The important point is that children learn that all problems can be addressed; nothing has to remain secret or hidden.

What should I do when the children come up with a solution that seems very unlikely to work?

The teacher helps the children to arrive at a workable solution and also to recognize that sometimes a solution has to be changed or another one tried.

During the meeting teachers can pose questions to help the children evaluate an idea and to consider different scenarios ("What if someone takes a really long turn and other people get tired of waiting?"). The challenge in thinking ahead like this is itself beneficial for children, and it often helps improve the solution the children work out. Not every solution has to work out beautifully. When teachers practice being non-judgmental and value children's ideas, the children learn something important when the first solution they decide on does not work and they have to modify or replace it—either on the spot or later in a class meeting.

Aren't class meetings with dual language learners confusing for young children?

Problem-solving interactions with dual language learners in a meeting are an excellent way for children to learn a second language.

Dual language learners quickly become familiar with commonly used phrases in both languages during class meetings. Acquiring the phrases and vocabulary of problem solving has real value and meaning to children; they realize it allows them to express their feelings directly to the other child involved in a conflict. They begin to learn the other language through purposeful use, not by memorizing words without a meaningful context. Refer back to pages 53–55 in Chapter 5 for more information.

References

Abramson, S. 2012. "Co-Inquiry: Documentation, Communication, Action." In *Our Inquiry, Our Practice: Undertaking, Supporting, and Learning From Early Childhood Research(ers)*, eds. G. Perry, B. Henderson, & D.R. Meier, 147–57. Washington, DC: NAEYC

Bredekamp, S., & C. Copple, eds. 1997. *Developmentally Appropriate Practice in Early Childhood Programs*. Rev. ed. Washington, DC: NAEYC.

Brophy, J.E. 2004. *Motivating Students to Learn*. 2nd ed. Mahwah, NJ: Lawrence Erlbaum Associates.

Bruno, H.E. 2011. "The Neurobiology of Emotional Intelligence: Using Our Brain to Stay Cool Under Pressure." *Young Children* 66 (1): 22–27.

Bullard, J., & J.R. Bullock. 2004. "Building Relationships Through Cooperative Learning." *Journal of Early Childhood Teacher Education* 25 (1): 39–48. doi: 10.1080/1090102040250107.

Carlsson-Paige, N., & D.E. Levin. 1998. *Before Push Comes to Shove: Building Conflict Resolution Skills With Children*. St. Paul, MN: Redleaf.

Coloroso, B. 2003. *The Bully, the Bullied, and the Bystander: From Preschool to High School: How Parents and Teachers Can Help Break the Cycle of Violence*. New York: Harper Resource.

Copple, C., & S. Bredekamp, eds. 2009. *Developmentally Appropriate Practice in Early Childhood Programs Serving Children From Birth Through Age 8*. 3rd ed. Washington, DC: NAEYC.

Decker, B. 1988. *The Art of Communicating: Achieving Interpersonal Impact in Business*. Los Altos, CA: Crisp Publications.

Derman-Sparks, L., & J. Olsen Edwards. 2010. *Anti-Bias Education for Young Children and Ourselves*. Washington, DC: NAEYC.

DeVries, R., & L. Kohlberg. 1990. *Constructivist Early Education: Overview and Comparison With Other Programs*. Washington, DC: NAEYC.

DeVries, R., & B. Zan. 1994. *Moral Classrooms, Moral Children: Creating a Constructivist Atmosphere in Early Education*. New York: Teachers College Press.

Dombro, A.L., J.R. Jablon, & C. Stetson. 2011. "Powerful Interactions." *Young Children* 66 (1): 12–16, 19–20. NAEYC: Washington, DC.

Gardner, H. 1983. *Frames of Mind: The Theory of Multiple Intelligences*. New York: Basic Books.

Gardner, H. 1993. *Multiple Intelligences: The Theory in Practice*. New York: Basic Books.

Gardner, H. 1999. *Intelligence Reframed: Multiple Intelligences for the 21st Century*. New York: Basic Books.

Gardner, H. 2006. *Multiple Intelligences: New Horizons.* New York: Basic Books.

Gartrell, D. 2006. "The Beauty of Class Meetings." Guidance Matters. *Young Children* 61 (6): 54–55.

Gartrell, D. 2014. *A Guidance Approach for the Encouraging Classroom.* 6th ed. Belmont, CA: Wadsworth/Cengage Learning.

Geake, J.G. 2009. *The Brain at School: Educational Neuroscience in the Classroom.* Open New York: University Press.

Glasser, W. 1969. *Schools Without Failure.* New York: Harper & Row.

Goleman, D. 2006. *Social Intelligence: The New Science of Human Relationships.* New York: Bantam.

González, N., L.C. Moll, & C. Amanti. 2005. *Funds of Knowledge: Theorizing Practices in Households, Communities, and Classrooms.* New York: Routledge.

Grant, K., & B.H. Davis. 2012. "Gathering Around." *Kappa Delta Pi Record,* 48 (3): 129–133.

Hannaford, C. 1995. *Smart Moves: Why Learning Is Not All in Your Head.* Arlington, VA: Great Ocean Publishers.

Harris, T., & Fuqua, D. 2000. "What Goes Around Comes Around: Building a Community of Learners." *Young Children 55 (*1): 44–47.

Jalongo, M. 1986. "Using Crisis-Oriented Books With Young Children." In *Reducing Stress in Young Children's Lives,* ed. J.B. McCracken, 29–36. Washington, DC: NAEYC.

Jalongo, M.R. 2008. *Learning to Listen, Listening to Learn: Building Essential Skills in Young Children.* Washington, DC: NAEYC.

Kataria, M. 2011. *Laugh for No Reason.* 4th ed. Mumbai, India: Madhuri International.

Katz, L.G., S.C., Chard, & Y. Kogan. forthcoming. *Engaging Children's Minds: The Project Approach.* 3rd ed. Westport, CT: Praeger.

Klein, A.J. 2003. "A Course on Children's Humor: A Model for Training Practitioners." In *Humor in Children's Lives: A Guidebook for Practitioners,* ed. A.J. Klein, 113–125. Westport, CT/London: Praeger.

Kohn, A. 2011. "The Case Against Grades." *Educational Leadership* 69 (3): 28–33.

Kreidler, W.J. 1994. *Teaching Conflict Resolution Through Children's Literature.* New York: Scholastic Professional Books.

Kreidler, W.J., & S.T. Whittall. 1999. *Adventures in Peacemaking: A Conflict Resolution Activity Guide for Early Childhood Educators.* 2nd ed. Cambridge, MA: Educators for Social Responsibility, and Boston: Work/Family Directions.

Levin, D. 2013. *Beyond Remote-Controlled Childhood: Teaching Young Children in the Media Age.* Washington, DC: NAEYC.

Lyon, C. 2006. "Humour and the Young Child." *Televizion* 19: 4–9.

McClurg, L.G. 1998. "Building an Ethical Community in the Classroom: Community Meeting." *Young Children 53* (2): 30–35.

Moll, L.C., & K. Whitmore. 1993. "Vygotsky in Educational Practice." In *Contexts for Learning: Sociocultural Dynamics in Children's Development*, eds. E. Forman, N. Minick, & C.A. Stone, 19–42. New York: Oxford.

Moorman, C. 2001. *Spirit Whisperers: Teachers Who Nurture a Child's Spirit.* Merrill, MI: Personal Power Press.

Moorman, C. 2003. "Teacher Talk: Nine Key Phrases That Help Motivate, Encourage, and Build Responsibility." *Instructor.* 36–39.

Nielsen, D.M. 2006. *Teaching Young Children: A Guide to Planning Your Curriculum, Teaching Learning Centers, and Just About Everything Else.* 2nd ed. Thousand Oaks, CA: Corwin Press.

Pelo, A., & F. Davidson. 2000. *That's Not Fair! A Teacher's Guide to Activism With Young Children.* St. Paul, MN: Redleaf.

Piaget, J. [1954] 1981. *Intelligence and Affectivity. Their Relationship During Child Development.* Ed. and trans. T.A. Brown & C.E. Kaegi. Palo Alto, CA: Annual Reviews.

Pirtle, S. 1998. *Linking Up!* Cambridge, MA: Educators for Social Responsibility.

Short, K.G., & J.C. Harste, With C. Burke. 1996. *Creating Classrooms for Authors and Inquirers.* 2nd ed. Portsmouth, NH: Heinemann.

Staal, D. 2008. *Words Kids Need to Hear: To Help Them Be Who God Made Them to Be.* Grand Rapids, MI: Zondervan.

Stipek, D.J. 1998. *Motivation to Learn: Integrating Theory and Practice.* New York: Viacom.

Styles, D. 2001. *Class Meetings: Building Leadership, Problem-Solving and Decision-Making Skills in the Respectful Classroom.* Markham, Ontario: Pembroke Publishers.

Taylor, M., A.B. Sachet, B.L. Maring, & A.M. Mannering. 2013. "The Assessment of Elaborated Role-Play in Young Children: Invisible Friends, Personified Objects, and Pretend Identities." *Social Development* 22 (1):75–93. doi:10.1111/sode.12011.

Vance, E. 2009. "Class Meetings: Teachers and Young Children Co-Constructing Problem Solving." PhD diss., University of Arizona.

Vance, E., & P.J. Weaver. 1995. *Class Meetings and More!* Tucson, AZ: Tortuga Press.

Whitin, P. 2001. "Kindness in a Jar." *Young Children* 56 (5): 18–22.

Wubbolding, R.E. 2007. "Glasser Quality School." *Group Dynamics: Theory, Research, and Practice* 11 (4): 253–261.

Yazigi, R., & P. Seedhouse. 2005. "'Sharing Time' With Young Learners." *TESL-EJ.* 9 (3): 1–26.

Acknowledgments

I greatly appreciate the students, parents, teachers, and administrators who have supported the implementation of class meetings throughout my years in education. You have immeasurably expanded my understanding of a facilitator's role with your trust and willingness to build community.

My sincere thanks to Patricia Jiménez Weaver for her expertise in developing our first two books. I extend a special thank you to principal Rosanna Gallagher for encouraging Patricia and me to write about the value of class meetings: You were the spark.

Let me acknowledge John and Donna Rabuck from the University of Arizona Writing Skills Program for their help during the writing of my doctoral thesis and review of this book. Also thanks to Barbara McNichol and Rosann Gomez, who helped me with final revisions.

My thanks to Dr. Sylvia C. Chard, a leading expert on the project approach.

Special thanks to Sara Van Slyke, director of Desert Spring Children's Center, and teachers Kathy Janssen and Christina Gutierrez for allowing me to work with the children on class meetings and laughter. I also thank Ethel Huerta and Charlie Danella at Tuller Elementary School.

To Dr. Mardan Kataria, thanks for opening my eyes to the importance of bringing joy and laughter into the learning environment.

To my mother Marilyn Wright, brother Doug Wright, late father Graham Wright, and to my children Jason and Jessica Vance. Thanks for all the beautiful loving support you have given me through all of my endeavors.

About the Author

Emily Vance, PhD, is an educator with more than 35 years' experience teaching young children as well as college and university methods and education courses. Vance earned a doctoral degree at the University of Arizona, conducting research that addresses teachers and young children co-constructing problem-solving strategies. She holds a National Board for Professional Teaching Standards credential, as well as Early Childhood and Bilingual Endorsements.

Vance's international experiences with class meetings in China, Portugal, England, and India have given her a global perspective. She works as a consultant to other educators about class meetings and about creating architectural environments to maximize learning.

Vance is a certified Laughter Yoga instructor and trainer, and she has incorporated techniques from this discipline in this book.

This is Vance's third book on class meetings with a focus on conflict resolution and problem-solving strategies. Her first book, *Class Meetings and More!* with Patricia Jiménez Weaver, was published in 1995. Their book *Class Meetings: Young Children Solving Problems Together* was published in 2002 by NAEYC.